WRITING
PSYCHOLOGICAL
REPORTS:
A GUIDE FOR CLINICIANS

Second Edition

Greg J. Wolber
and
William F. Carne

Professional Resource Press
Sarasota, Florida

Published by Professional Resource Press
(An imprint of Professional Resource Exchange, Inc.)
Post Office Box 15560
Sarasota, FL 34277-1560

This publication is sold with the understanding that the Publisher is not engaged in
rendering professional services. If legal, psychological, medical, accounting, or other
expert advice or assistance is sought or required, the reader should seek the services of
a competent professional.

The copy editor for this book was Patricia Rockwood, the cover designer was Jami
Stinnet, the managing editor was Debbie Fink, and the production coordinator was
Laurie Girsch.

Library of Congress Cataloging-in-Publication Data

Wolber, Greg J., date.
    Writing psychological reports : a guide for clinicians / Greg J. Wolber and William F.
Carne.-- 2nd ed.
      p. cm.
    Includes bibliographical references and index.
    ISBN 1-56887-076-0 (alk. paper)
    1. Psychodiagnostics. 2. Report writing. 3. Clinical psychology--Authorship. I. Carne,
William F. - II. Title

RC469.W58 2002
616.89'075--dc21

                                                 2002068389

DEDICATION

This book is dedicated to the memory of William F. Carne, Sr.

Greg J. Wolber and
William F. Carne

PREFACE TO THE
SECOND EDITION

This Second Edition of *Writing Psychological Reports: A Guide for Clinicians* offers several changes from the First Edition (Wolber & Carne, 1993). While the suggested format for a psychological evaluation remains essentially unchanged, modifications have been made within sections of the format which are thought to enhance the quality of the evaluation. A short section concerning the *Notification of Purpose and Limits of Confidentiality* has been added as well as a breakdown of the *Background Information* section into subsections. More emphasis is placed on the integration of collateral information into the report along with a discussion of what information should and should not be included. Many new examples are provided to supplement and clarify the narrative descriptions of the text and a new example of a full report is provided. Cognitive-behavioral concepts have been integrated into the text. Finally, the *Recommendations* section has been modified to incorporate specific strengths and problem areas. A model is presented for incorporating areas of focus into recommendations wherein each area is discussed individually relevant to its current status and importance to the psychological functioning of the subject. Examples of specific management strategies to address problem areas and to incorporate areas of strengths into recommendations are presented.

TABLE OF
CONTENTS

INTRODUCTION

The objective of this text is to present a structured format for writing a psychological report. A single report format is presented with an explanation of the content for each section of the format. The authors recognize that there are many different ways to write a psychological report, and clinicians must take into account the unique set of needs for each assessment.

The method presented here is not meant to be seen as superior to other report formats. Many reports may require specialized formats that are quite different from this one (e.g., competency to stand trial, criminal responsibility, disability determination, and psychoeducational evaluations). Courts, schools, hospitals, and other agencies requesting evaluations may have a significant influence on the format and content of the report. However, for the general psychological report, which is requested to determine "psychological functioning," we have found this format to be widely accepted. For those reports that do require a specialized focus, many of the concepts presented here may prove helpful.

This book is not intended to describe test administration, scoring, or interpretation. Nor is it intended to describe how one goes about obtaining collateral and interview data for the psychological report. Obviously these are important, for without quality assessment and interpretation, the final product, the report, would have little, if any, value.

Chapter 1, "Before Beginning," addresses some major issues that we feel should be considered prior to initiating the report. The remaining chapters describe a structured format for a psychological report and outline the essential clinical content for the various sections of the report. Although the information provided here is intended primarily for students or beginning report writers, more experienced clinicians may also find it helpful.

WRITING PSYCHOLOGICAL REPORTS:
A GUIDE FOR CLINICIANS

Second Edition

Chapter 1

BEFORE BEGINNING

RATIONALE FOR A REPORT

In the literature and among clinicians, there is some disagreement as to the usefulness of psychological reports (Ownby, 1991). However, we believe a well-developed and well-written psychological report provides referents and others with a coherent means to convey, with some sense of objectivity, the intellectual, cognitive, behavioral, emotional, and dynamic functioning of an individual. The psychological evaluation provides the mental health practitioner with an in-depth view of the subject that is probably unequaled by other forms of evaluation.

The report is comparable to the physician's MRI (Magnetic Resonance Imagery) in its capacity to provide an in-depth analysis of the personality and to "see" beyond the manifest level. The well-written psychological report can assist in clarifying conflicts and explain overt behavior. It can describe the interaction of intellectual and personality factors and assist with differential diagnoses. The well-written psychological evaluation provides a normative comparison of the functioning of the individual with its integration of relatively objective data and clinical expertise. The end product of the psychological report is a set of hypotheses and conclusions (results) concerning the subject and, where appropriate, suggested means to address these results (i.e., recommendations).

Psychological evaluations are used by the courts, hospitals, counselors, social workers, educational institutions, government agencies, and others to make crucial decisions about peoples' lives, and they can play a significant role in the direction those lives might take. Dr. William Menninger made the following comment over 50 years ago during his tenure as President of the American Psychiatric Association: "The diagnostic function of the clinical psychologist is well established . . . that the competent psychiatrist . . . would no more exclude the special techniques of the psychologist in his studies than would the capable internist exclude the findings of the roentgenologist [radiologist]" (Menninger, 1948, pp. 389-390).

Some clinicians find it acceptable to present only the raw data or make a phone call providing a verbal interpretation of their findings, but we believe this is insufficient and deprives the subject and those who work with him or her of a valuable product. Although this may be appropriate in a minority of cases, it is the premise of this text that the psychological evaluation process deserves a well-conceptualized psychological report.

FUNDAMENTAL GUIDELINES

Experienced clinicians likely follow a format in developing their reports. This may be a mental image or an actual on-paper outline of the contents for the report. In the latter case, notes taken from test results and other sources of relevant information can be placed in the outline under the appropriate content area to facilitate writing or dictation. We believe that this structured approach to writing the report is imperative, for it helps assure that certain content areas are always covered, or at least considered. In addition, the defensive posture of some subjects tends to deter the evaluator from certain areas of the personality that should be explored. Using a predetermined list of areas to consider should result in a more comprehensive and useful report than when no structure is followed. Although some clinicians may be able to develop a good report without a structured format, we suggest that this is not appropriate for the novice psychologist or student.

This does not mean that the writer cannot stray from the format when individual variations are relevant. Certainly no format should be considered exhaustive or always appropriate to the specific assessment at hand. Reports must be tailored to the unique findings of each patient or subject and to the needs of the referent. Certainly specialization will require specific content that may or may not be part of the format. Although the content presented in the format suggested in this text may prove helpful to most clinicians, modification to fit individual needs is certainly encouraged. Whether or not the report writer uses the format presented here, modifies it, or develops his or her own, a predetermined structure to writing the psychological report is recommended. We continue to employ a written format and believe that this is beneficial even for experienced clinicians. Others support this position (Ownby, 1997; Tallent, 1993).

Of fundamental importance in writing the psychological report is the referral question. Weiner (1985) found that users of psychological reports favored those reports that explicitly addressed the referral question. If the clinician performing the assessment has not adequately considered or does not understand the basic question asked by the referent, the report will likely not provide what has been requested. Not addressing the referral question is ignoring the referent's perceived needs and may result not only in a misguided report but also in ill feelings between the referent and the report writer. However, sometimes the referral question was not the most appropriate question, or perhaps other questions should have been asked along with the referral question. As an example, the referral question may be "Patient exhibits mental confusion and forgetfulness. Please determine personality factors that may be etiological." An experienced clinician would recognize that a better question would include the possibility of organic origin. For most assessments, giving the referral source more than has been requested would likely be considered appropriate. However, this is not always the case; for example, when the content of a report should be restricted as in certain court-ordered evaluations.

Related to the issue of answering the referral question is what to do when the conclusions, or lack thereof, do not provide an answer to the referral question. Do we give our best guess based on what data we have? We believe this is inappropriate. The report writer should not force a choice at the expense of overstating the facts. If you don't know, then you don't know. Admit the ignorance and go forward with attempting to provide possible alternatives or suggestions for how the question might be answered. There is nothing wrong with reporting difficulty with answering the referral question or that there is a lack of clarity from the assessment as to the clinical state of the subject.

Any report, psychological or otherwise, should take into consideration the audience it addresses and the setting in which it is performed (Hartlage & Merck, 1971; Harvey, 1997; Jones & Gross, 1959). If our audience cannot understand what we have written, what good is the report? This consideration has several implications. The report writer would likely vary the language and the manner by which results are presented depending on the intended recipient of the report. For example, a report written to a probation officer would likely be different from that written to a psychiatrist. Within the mental health field, there will be differences in reports written to various professionals (e.g., psychiatry, social work, etc.), although most mental health professionals should understand many of the concepts and language used by the psychologist. Even within the profession of psychology, differences in reports may be helpful, depending on the theoretical orientation and training of the reader. Sometimes it may be appropriate for different persons, with varying degrees and types of expertise, to review the report. The report writer may want to consider the idea of the "lowest common denominator" as the audience of the report. The writer should not compromise needed expert opinion and technical concepts when they are germane to understanding the subject; however, the report may need to provide more explanation so technical ideas can be more readily comprehended.

The following three methods are not recommended for writing psychological reports: (a) a "test-by-test" presentation, (b) "single-test reporting," and (c) "blind interpretation." The first involves one test and its interpretation followed by another test and its interpretation. The second develops a report from a single source of data (e.g., one test) and supports an often simplistic and incomplete perception of the personality as having only one dimension. The third involves direct interpretation from test data only, without consideration of other information such as the interview of the subject and collateral data. These forms of report writing do not represent a consolidation of the data across tests and other sources of information and likely indicate either a problem with conceptualizing personality dynamics or a lack of knowledge about personality functioning. Although these methods may seem like an easy way to write a report for the neophyte clinician, in the long run, they often do not incorporate the knowledge of the writer and do not present an integrated view of the subject. However, there may exist circumstances for which a single test interpretation is appropriate or necessary. For example, a school may have a need for a screening assessment consisting of an intelligence test. Another frequently encountered example of this is the report written from the results of the Minnesota Multiphasic Personality Inventory-2 (MMPI-2; Hathaway & McKinley, 1989). This may be appropriate if the report is an attempt to screen for certain pathology or is to be used for research purposes. However, to call this a comprehensive psychological evaluation is an injustice to the psychological report. Most experienced clinicians would agree that projective assessment is capable of tapping dimensions of the personality different from that which is measured by most so-called "objective instruments" such as the MMPI-2. The psychological report should represent a synthesis of the data not only across testing, but also through the integration of behavioral observations and collateral information such as relevant social history. Even when a single test is employed (which we discourage), integration with subject presentation and collateral data is essential.

"Blind analysis" may be appropriate for training purposes but not for a psychological evaluation on a real subject. By "blind analysis," we mean the administration of tests with direct interpretation from the test data and without consideration of the behavioral/emotional presentation of the subject or of information from other sources. This may even extend to the questionable practice of developing a psychological report solely from test data that someone else administered without interviewing the subject or considering collateral data. Even IQ scores, which are often considered to be more "objective" than the results of personality instruments, especially projectives, can be misleading. The effects of medication, motivation, a thought disorder, and/or variation from standard test administration and assessment conditions can have a profound impact on test performance. Psychological tests are tools that point clinicians in a specific direction but by no means provide the final word. Interpretation does not come from a test but from the clinician responsible for the evaluation. The clinician must come between the assessment data and the final report.

Another frequently encountered problem with psychological reports is the use of codes, statistics, and formulas that have little, if any, meaning, to the reader. Often the report will employ "clinical shorthand" that leaves the reader struggling with interpretation. One example of this is the "codes" sometimes reported by clinicians who use the MMPI-2. Such a code might read something like 2'4735/6822"19-0/:L'FK. How would a psychiatrist, social worker, or other mental health professional react to a report that includes this? Although it may be appropriate to include this if the report is going to another psychologist who uses this same system of coding, a written description of the findings of the report should also be included. At some point the report may appropriately fall in the hands of others who could find a good psychological evaluation valuable but would not be able to understand it because of the code. Other examples include complicated ratios or abbreviations. Esoteric reporting of this nature usually does little service to anyone. Imagine the reaction of the reader who is unfamiliar with Exner's System of Rorschach (Rorschach, 1948) interpretation and comes across the statement in a psychological report as follows: "On the Rorschach, the subject scored a WSUM6 of 4" (Exner, 1986). Even the reporting of subtest scores from the Wechsler can be confusing and misleading without integrative interpretation. This does not mean that we do not consider statistics and formulas; however, these should be a component of the interpretive process and not the final interpretation itself. To inappropriately use these "clinical shorthands" defies good report writing.

Psychological evaluations are not social histories and should not be dominated by social history material. However, the material provided by relevant social history and other sources of collateral data, such as behavior observations by others, may be as relevant as the data gleaned from the tests themselves. The social history tends to tell the subject's life story and how others see him or her functioning. The psychological report takes this information, along with test data, and weaves it into a clinical picture of the individual consistent with his or her overt life. The same is true concerning the mental status exam. Although the psychological report should integrate the results of the mental status examination, the mental status exam should not dominate the report.

The length and typing of the report deserves consideration. As with most products, length does not necessarily correlate with quality (Tallent, 1980). Also, length will vary with the type and unique needs of the report. We have found around four to six pages to be the average length for a general comprehensive report using the format included in this text. Although the length of the report may vary, it is doubtful that justification can be given to a comprehensive psychological evaluation in one or two pages. We suggest the report be single spaced with two blank spaces between sections. Bold-face print should be used to set off the different sections. Neatness and uniformity of typing and formatting is important, and correctness of syntax, spelling, and grammar cannot be overemphasized. We suggest the report be written in the third person singular from the perspective of the assessment itself (e.g., "This assessment indicates. . . ."). Use of subjective language or obvious personal opinion should be avoided. We continue to see reports that describe the subject as "attractive" or that include statements made that represent an emotional reaction (likely transference) on the part of the writer (e.g., "Unfortunately this helpless child continues to suffer from feelings of depression"). Although the compassion of such a statement may be warranted, it represents bias and should be avoided in the report.

Concurrent with quality should come timeliness. We consider this issue as one of the most important logistical concerns facing any profession. If either quality or timeliness is missing, the value of the report is diminished. Different settings and referents generally have different time criteria for the submission of the report. Generally, reports should be sent to the referent as soon as possible after the referral is made. To not respond in a timely manner is discourteous; however, timely reporting should not come at the expense of the quality of the report. One common complaint, often bestowed on those who write psychological reports, is "The patient will be long gone before we get the results of the psychological report." An example of a circumstance that could cause delays in completing an evaluation is a subject who "is too psychotic" to participate in the assessment or does not fully cooperate with the evaluation. If it becomes necessary to exceed the due date for the evaluation, the referent deserves the courtesy of a phone call explaining the circumstances and a projected date for completion. Sometimes it may be necessary to provide the referent with whatever the report writer can legitimately organize before all the relevant information has been collected and considered. This is acceptable if the reporting clinician provides clear statements of (a) the limitations of the data and (b) assurance that, if more relevant information becomes available, the report will be updated. The referent should be informed of any relevant outstanding information that could be potentially important to the assessment results.

CONFIDENTIALITY AND ETHICS

The issues of confidentiality and ethics are important considerations in the writing of the psychological report. The psychological report is generally a confidential document; therefore, clinicians involved with this document must adhere to legal and ethical standards of confidentiality. The consumer must be safeguarded against undue or inappropriate disclosure. It is suggested that the reader review the "Ethical Principles of Psychologists and Code of Ethics" (American Psychological Association, 1992) regarding confidentiality and ethics. In addition, the report writer should be aware of, and familiar with, organizational/institutional standards, as well as other local standards pertaining to psychological reports. State departments of mental health and other agencies will often provide statutory codes governing confidential documents on request.

The inclusion of irrelevant information that could invade privacy or be degrading to the subject or others should be avoided. For example, it is neither appropriate nor necessary to reveal in the report that the subject had an extramarital affair while in a previous marriage if this adds little to the purpose of the report. Also information concerning persons other than the subject should be safeguarded, and use of the actual name of the person may not be necessary. For example, it would be inappropriate to state in the psychological report "The subject is currently involved in a sexual relationship with a coworker named John Smith." The report would be just as useful if the name of the coworker were omitted. Consideration could also be given to the appropriateness and relevance of the use of the word "coworker." The report writer might consider providing such information verbally (when necessary and with permission of the subject) or excluding it altogether. The referent may not be the only person who, for one reason or another, will have access to the psychological report (Harvey, 1997). Over time, evaluations can gain a wide and varied audience. Protection from inappropriate disclosure or unnecessary invasion of privacy, though not always possible, starts with the initiator of the evaluation.

As indicated in this text, our format uses the heading "Confidential Psychological Evaluation" as one means of addressing the issue. We have added to our format a section addressing notification of the subject by the evaluator concerning the limits of confidentiality as well as the purpose of the report.

COMPUTERIZATION

Contemporary psychological assessment has come to rely more and more on computerization. Frequently tests are administered, scored, and interpreted by computer software. This is both good and bad. Computers are valuable assets in the administration and scoring of psychological assessment, although problems can arise with the use of computerization during these phases of the assessment process. We have reviewed evaluations where the report of two different subjects had been erroneously merged, through word processing software, into one report. Of frequent concern is the use of computer interpretation of data which is often actuarially based and not clinical judgment. Although computer-generated information can be helpful in formulating hypotheses about what might be going on with a subject, it should never be used as the conclusion. This is even true of so-called "objective tests" such as the Wechsler scales (Wechsler, 1974, 1989, 1997). No score should stand alone without the clinical judgment and experience of the clinician involved in drawing conclusions. Matarazzo (1983, 1986a, 1986b) warned of the dangers involved in this process. Ownby (1991) also questions the validity of computerized testing. Although Fowler and Butcher (1986) tend to be more supportive, they too voice the need for safeguards with computerized interpretation. The final responsibility for the psychological evaluation lies in the hands of the person who signs the report, and not the developer of interpretive software. Computers can be helpful and serve as another source of external data or opinion, but if used inappropriately, they can leave out the most important element of the report: an integrative interpretation. As Ownby (1991) states, "Under no circumstances should a computer interpretation be included in a report unless it is clearly supported by assessment data or clearly labeled as speculation" (p. 148).

THE REPORT WRITER

The experience and training of the report writer are primary factors in the writing of the psychological report. Psychologists or trainees with little experience should receive close supervision when writing a psychological report. Psychology has long supported a strong supervisory model, and constructive criticism should both be sought and provided without reservation. The subtle issues involved in working with human subjects, such as transference, projective identification, and value bias, are powerful influences, and the input from a somewhat removed third party can be extremely valuable. Review by a third party can catch potential problems with interpretation and content as well as point out mistakes such as typographical errors, which can impact the meaning of findings. For example, not having the word "no" in front of the term "suicidal ideation" when it was meant to be there is an obviously serious omission. The report writer is the key to the quality of the psychological report. The consolidation and integration of psychological test data, behavioral observations, and collateral information, including relevant social history, rely on the report writer and whatever additional resources (e.g., supervision) are available.

Robert Carson (1990) states, "More generally, I believe that particular individuals when working with particular assessment instruments, typically those to which they have devoted much study and in the use of which they have acquired vast experience, are capable of assessment performances that far exceed the standard for the instrument" (p. 439). Knowledge of personality theory and psychopathology are crucial, not just expertise in psychological tests. Dr. Carson draws an appropriate analogy. He states that to talk about the validity of a test is like talking about the validity of the stethoscope. The conclusions drawn in the psychological report acquire their validity from the report writer, not just from the instruments employed.

THE ORGANIZATION OF THE REPORT

Specified formats for psychological reports are not a novel concept. Mayman (1959), in an article entitled "Style, Focus, Language and Content of an Ideal Psychological Test Report," described in detail personality factors, such as ego defenses, that the author believed should be included in a psychological report. Earlier, Lodge (1953) suggested an outline to help students write psychological reports. Klopher (1960) suggested that the report should be broken down into four sections: (a) reason for referral, (b) general observations, (c) test interpretation, and (d) summary. Others (Applebaum, 1972; Axelrod, 2000; Hollis & Donn, 1979; Wolber, 1980) suggest more complex formats. Ownby (1991) and Tallent (1980) have been more reluctant to describe specific content, citing the need for variation in the report as a function of the referral question, setting, and subject type. As indicated earlier, specialized reports may require specialized formats depending on need (Weiner, 1999). Modifications may be necessary in any report format depending on the unique circumstances involved.

Below is an outline for the suggested format. The different sections of the outline are discussed in detail in this text. The format presented here seems relatively consistent with formats suggested in the past and may be helpful in a variety of settings with different referral questions and subject types. It is not meant to be exhaustive. We suggest that report writers consider all areas of the outline when writing their reports.

The suggested format includes the following sections:

 I.   REPORT HEADING AND DEMOGRAPHIC INFORMA-
      TION
 II. REASON FOR REFERRAL
 III. NOTIFICATION OF PURPOSE AND LIMITS OF CONFI-
      DENTIALITY
 IV. EVALUATION INSTRUMENTS AND SOURCES OF IN-
      FORMATION
 V.   BACKGROUND INFORMATION
 VI. BEHAVIORAL OBSERVATIONS
 VII. ASSESSMENT RESULTS
      A. INTELLECTUAL AND COGNITIVE FUNCTIONING
      B. PERSONALITY FUNCTIONING
         1. EMOTIONAL FACTORS
         2. INTRAPSYCHIC
         3. INTERPERSONAL
      C. IMPRESSIONS
 VIII. SUMMARY AND RECOMMENDATIONS

A complete outline of the format with suggested questions to be answered under each section is included in Appendices A (pp. 105-112) and B (pp. 113-119). The evaluation format has blank lines under each section title for handwritten notes. Appendix C (pp. 121-131) provides an example of a psychological report using the suggested format.

Chapter 2

PRERESULTS SECTIONS

REPORT HEADING AND
DEMOGRAPHIC INFORMATION

The report heading or title should be placed at the top of the first page of the report, followed by a listing of subject demographics and other relevant information to provide a brief description of the subject. The heading is usually centered and set off in larger and bolder type than the text of the report. The heading should be reflective of the type of report. Specialized reports may require a specific title that reflects the purpose of those reports (e.g., competency to stand trial or psychoeducational evaluations). For the general psychological report, the heading may be something like *Confidential Psychological Evaluation* or *Confidential Psychological Assessment.* Although some clinicians may feel that the word *confidential* is redundant because it should be understood that the title *psychological evaluation* means the report is to be considered confidential, we believe the report should be clearly designated as protected. Therefore, we consider it appropriate to include the word *confidential* in the title. However, if not included in the title, the report should be clearly marked *confidential.* A statement on the first page regarding prohibitions on rerelease may also be desirable.

Identifying information is also important to the report. Enough demographic information should be listed to allow the reader to identify the subject, thus avoiding any mistakes in identification, and also provide the reader with a brief and quick overview of the basics about the subject. Identifying information can also provide clues about clinical issues for comparison with assessment data. For example, the fact that the client is 80 years old as opposed to 6 may have implications concerning etiology of cognitive confusion and the possibility of dementia. Identifying information should minimally include (a) name, (b) date of birth, (c) sex, (d) marital status, (e) school grade or occupational status, (f) date(s) of evaluation, and (g) referral source(s). The school grade or occupation can be important for comparison with assessment results (e.g., a brain surgeon who scores an IQ of 80 or a 10th grader who scores on the 3rd-grade level on a reading achievement test). We also prefer to include the age of the subject, in addition to the birth date, for the convenience of the reader. In hospital settings, report writers may want to also include the admission date. Other reports may include information about the subject relevant to the location or referral source of the evaluation. For example, if the assessment is conducted within a school system for psychoeducational purposes, the identifying information may include the name of the school. For forensic evaluations, the name of the court of jurisdiction might be included.

Optional information could include a medical record or case number, the name and title of the report writer and others who assisted with the assessment, and the name of professionals closely associated with the subject and involved in the referral (e.g., subject's therapist or admitting psychiatrist). Anything that the writer feels is appropriate for this section can be included; however, we suggest that only enough demographic/identifying information be used to meet the purpose of the evaluation. An exhaustive list could cover the whole first page. We recommend that the list be confined to the top one-third and placed under the title starting in the left-hand margin. We also suggest that two columns be used, if necessary, to conserve space.

REASON FOR REFERRAL

This is the first narrative section of the report. Sometimes it is titled *Source and Reason for Referral, Chief Complaint,* or *Presenting Problem.* We feel that *Chief Complaint* or *Presenting Problem* does not accurately describe the purpose of this section and that such information may be more appropriate for the *Background Information* section of the report. We suggest the term *Reason for Referral.* This section should include the source of the referral as well as the reason for the referral. Of course, this will vary according to the actual originator of the referral and the referral question. The section *Reason for Referral* should minimally include the following:

1.   From whom and where the subject was referred.
2.   The reason for the requested evaluation and, where appropriate, the referral question itself.

Although this section is generally brief, it is an extremely important section of the report. It represents the central issue to be addressed and therefore should be reflective of this. Somewhere in the report, the referral question should be answered, and, as the writer is composing the report, he or she should have in mind what the referral source is requesting. An example of the *Reason for Referral* section follows:

> Mrs. X was referred for psychological evaluation by John Smith, MD, the subject's treating psychiatrist. Dr. Smith requested psychological evaluation in order to assist with differential diagnosis between depression with psychotic features and schizophrenia. Mrs. X has exhibited marked symptoms of depression as well as auditory hallucinations.

As can be seen in the preceding example, a very brief description of the symptoms exhibited by the subject that likely motivated the referral is included. Although this is appropriate and useful in understanding the referral question, it also represents clinical data that should be presented and likely expanded upon elsewhere in the report. Extended descriptions of symptoms are not recommended for this section, for such details can begin to look like a clinical interpretation of the subject more appropriately reported in other sections. Also, this section should concisely tell the reader the reason for the referral and allow him or her to quickly move on to the assessment findings. In the majority of cases, three to five sentences should be sufficient to adequately describe why the clinician has been asked to evaluate the subject; however, if more elaboration is needed, then it should be included.

Although the referral question is most often the focus of the evaluation, other important areas may emerge concerning the psychological functioning of the subject, and they should certainly be mentioned in the report. Most referral sources appreciate this broader perspective. For example, in the course of evaluating a subject to assist with differential diagnosis between depression with psychotic features and schizophrenia, one discovers signs of possible brain damage; this would certainly be included in the report. For this reason, most clinicians, although asked a specific question, will assess more broadly, minimally covering certain predetermined areas. On the other hand, we have experienced referents who have said "I don't want all that other stuff. I just want to know. . . ." Probably it is better to give too much information than too little. Remember to try to *address the referral question if at all possible.*

As mentioned in Chapter 1, sometimes it is difficult to determine just what the referral question is. Not infrequently a referent will ask for only a "psychological evaluation"; in this case some exploration with the referent is not only preferred but necessary. Secondary benefits may result from this approach. Not only can the evaluator gain some clear direction for the purpose of the evaluation, but he or she can also gain valuable background information about the subject; this may be relevant data that can contribute to results. We have also experienced the referral question "I don't know what is going on with this person; can you help me find out?" and the referent, when contacted for clarification, remains very vague because he or she just does not have any idea about the specifics of the request. In this case, the reason for referral can be reflective of this vagueness and may include something like, "Dr. Smith requested evaluation in order to assist with clarifying Mrs. X's psychological functioning." It is important to keep in mind, when exploring with a referral source, not to develop a preconceived idea of what the referral source desires for an outcome. Report writing should never be a matter of "tell them what they want to hear" but should be a process of objective reporting to the extent possible.

In some cases, the **Reason for Referral** should be more or less inclusive depending on the unique needs of the assessment. For example, for court ordered evaluations, we generally cite the court of jurisdiction and the judge who wrote the order. We also include the code section under which the order was written, if there is one. This makes clear the specific purpose of the report and that the report is, to some extent, governed by the cited statute. Other examples might include a request for an educational evaluation under a specific federal or state standard, an evaluation requested for disability determination, or an assessment for worker's compensation purposes. Each unique referral situation should be reflected in the *Reason for Referral* section.

NOTIFICATION OF PURPOSE AND
LIMITS OF CONFIDENTIALITY

Prior to initiating the assessment process, the evaluator should provide the subject with information concerning the purpose of the report and the limits of confidentiality. Sometimes this may not be possible; some subjects may be of such mental condition that they cannot understand what has been explained or cannot fully comprehend the possible uses of the report. In such cases, the ethical and legal implications of not providing notification should be considered. Because these can vary from individual to individual and from setting to setting, each circumstance may require different approaches (e.g., a court ordered evaluation versus an outpatient assessment for a man whose therapist wants to know more about the subject's depression). Whatever the circumstances surrounding the notification, a statement that this was either completed or attempted including a description of the subject's response and other related information, is recommended for the psychological report.

Some report writers will include a notification statement in the *Behavioral Observations* section of the report, given that this section describes some of the relevant communication between the subject and the evaluator. We suggest a separate section for the notification statement toward the beginning of the report. A short statement that this was completed can also be included in the *Behavioral Observations* section if this helps clarify the interaction between the subject and the evaluator. We suggest this section be entitled *Notification of Purpose and Limits of Confidentiality.* An example is as follows:

The purpose of the evaluation and limits of confidentiality were explained to Mr. Patient. He was told that a report concerning his psychological functioning would be developed and sent to his therapist, Dr.

H. E. Goode. Mr. Patient indicated that he understood
and agreed to participate in the assessment process.

EVALUATION INSTRUMENTS AND
SOURCES OF INFORMATION

This section lists all tests and other sources of information used in
the assessment process. Test titles should be spelled out in full, and, if
they are cited in abbreviated form in the text of the report, the listed
test should be followed by the abbreviation used for the test. For example, if the Wechsler Adult Intelligence Scale-Third Edition
(Wechsler, 1997) is listed it can be followed by "WAIS-III." Only the
abbreviation need be used thereafter. If modifications in the test administration are made during the assessment (e.g., only completing
part of a test because the subject refused to finish), these should be
described. Interviews with the subject should also be listed with the
name of the subject and the date(s) interviewed, for example: "Clinical Interview with John Patient on March 10th, 2001." Collateral information or data from sources not involving direct contact with the
subject should also be included (e.g., previous psychological evaluations, reports from other disciplines, interviews with family or friends,
consultations with other professionals). The list of collateral sources
of information can be extensive in some cases. The evaluation instru-
ments/sources of information used can be listed in one column starting
at the left-hand margin or in paragraph form for those who wish to
conserve space.

BACKGROUND INFORMATION

Background information is extremely important and can provide
the life story into which results of psychological testing are integrated.
For example, when the tests provide signs of possible organic involvement and the history of the subject reveals that he or she began to
experience problems with frustration and memory last year, these two
facts, taken together, can provide a plausible hypothesis for the subject's
behavior. The link between test data and real life is vital for the evaluation to have practical application. Background information can help

provide this link, but it should not dominate the report or the report could evolve into a social history rather than a psychological evaluation. Filling the psychological report with unnecessary background information avoids the more complicated, but appropriate, task of developing an integrated psychological picture of the subject.

Sometimes this section is referred to as *Relevant History* or *Relevant Information*; however, we believe the term *Background Information* more accurately defines the purpose of the section. We suggest that the *Background Information* section generally be no more than one page of the report, although this may vary. It is important not to limit this section to predetermined content; the *Background Information* section should include any information that is relevant to the evaluation. We suggest that, at minimum, the following content areas should be considered:

1. ***Subject Demographics and Developmental History.*** Subject demographics in a one-line, concise statement including the subject's name, age, race, marital status, and sex. If birth was normal or complicated, and if any developmental problems existed. History of any sexual/physical abuse.

2. ***Familial History and Significant Relationships.*** Family constellation and general relationships with family members, past and current. Marriage issues and significant other relationships. Current and relevant past living arrangements.

3. ***Education and Employment History.*** Level of education and any special education services or learning disability along with grades received. Work history and job-related difficulties. Any disability status or worker's compensation issues. Military service and discharge status.

4. ***Medical and Psychiatric History.*** Serious or chronic medical problems (e.g., head injury) and psychiatric history to include inpatient and outpatient treatment, treatment outcome, and diagnoses given. Description of symptoms.

5. ***Alcohol and Drug History.*** Current and past use to include type of substance, frequency, and amounts. Impact on functioning and treatment efforts.

6. ***Other Relevant History.*** Legal history, interpersonal issues, sexual history, avocational pursuits, and any other relevant history.

7. ***Factors Prompting Referral.*** Type of behavior/circumstances that prompted the evaluation: A more comprehensive description than that which was presented in the ***Reason for Referral*** section.

Some report writers may prefer to label each section according to its specific content, as above, while others incorporate the above content in three or four paragraphs. The former method may help readers organize their thinking as they read. Titled content areas help assure that the report will include, or at least consider, these areas for inclusion. The writer should not limit the content to those specific areas if other information is relevant. Also, areas can overlap and there are no hard and fast rules about what should be included under which section. Certain areas may be emphasized more than others depending on the focus and purpose of the report. For example, an evaluation performed on an adolescent may place more emphasis on education and family issues than an evaluation performed on an adult.

Although it may be considered redundant to repeat demographic information already included at the beginning of the report, we suggest that the report do so in one concise sentence at the onset of this section. For example, this sentence could read "Jane Patient is a 47-year-old, African-American married female." This one sentence reveals who the subject is and provides a brief mental image of the subject. Specific physical characteristics, such as height and weight, should be left for the ***Behavioral Observations*** section of the report. Any complication with birth or meeting age-appropriate developmental milestones should be mentioned. Issues of early childhood abuse can be mentioned here as well as other relevant information about the family of origin. The nature of familial relationships and issues of marriage, separation, and divorce are also mentioned in this section as well as parent-child conflicts and sibling issues.

Another paragraph or subsection should include a description of the subject's educational background, performance in school, and vocational history. Certainly the fact that the subject was, or is, in special educational services or has been diagnosed as learning disabled is important content which will have implications for interpreting test data and making recommendations. Educational level and academic performance can be compared with IQ and other test results to assist in determining if subjects are under- or overachieving. Work history is also important and can provide clues about level of functioning. The type of work the subject has performed or currently performs can be very helpful in determining if there has been a deterioration in functioning. For example, a college professor would not normally score an IQ of 70. Emotional/psychological factors can also have a significant impact on work performance. Education and functioning in school, as well as work performance, can represent strengths and weaknesses to be integrated into the report.

The medical and psychiatric history of the subject deserves particular attention. In providing information about medical issues, it is important that the report writer cite the source of the information provided. This may be a statement such as "John Patient's medical record from Hospital X stated that he has had four seizures in the past 7 months." It is probably important to make reference to the source of all medical information so the reader is aware that what is said is not the writer's conclusion about the subject but was taken from a specific source. Medical difficulties such as tumors, head injury, seizures, thyroid problems, diabetes, abnormal blood pressure, and so on all can affect the psychological functioning of the subject and should be mentioned. However, it is important to remember that psychologists are not medical doctors. Medical information that is not backed up by trained medical professionals should be described as being of questionable validity, and the source of the information should be cited.

Obviously, the psychiatric history of the subject is important and can provide valuable information about the subject's psychological functioning. Hospitalizations for psychiatric reasons should be included along with discharge diagnoses. Outpatient treatment should also be included, as well as, where available, the reason for treatment. Symptoms described in hospital/therapy records may also be helpful. Medications that have been prescribed, and impressions by medical professionals of the helpfulness of medications to the subject, can have significant implications for both treatment and diagnosis. The subject's record of compliance with treatment, including adherence to a medication regimen, is potentially valuable information for the *Background Information* section.

Often serious mental health problems coexist with substance abuse/dependence. This is one area that is frequently not explored to the extent necessary given the denial level of many people involved with drugs and/or alcohol. An alcohol/drug history should be taken even if only to rule out any use/abuse in this area. This should minimally state the type, frequency, and amount of use, treatment efforts, and impact of use on subject's functioning. Because many traditional psychological test batteries do not include a separate instrument to evaluate this area, assessment of alcohol/drug issues is often obtained during the clinical interview and included in the *Background Information* section of the report. If specialized assessment seems warranted, then referral for such should be part of the *Recommendations.* The role that alcohol/drugs play within the subject's defensive structure (e.g., escape from unpleasant feelings, self-medicating, disinhibiting impulses) can be included in the *Personality Functioning* section of the report.

An area that is often avoided in the psychological evaluation is that of sexual history/problems. This may be the result of the subject's guardedness, embarrassment, or the psychologist's fear of offending the subject. Questions about sexual practices and feelings may not be easy to address, but when crucial to the psychological functioning of the subject, these areas must be explored. As with drug and alcohol involvement, information on sexual issues can be stated in the *Background Information* section of the report and may be integrated into the *Personality Functioning* section to the degree this information contributes to personality dynamics. This information may also be an important component of the *Recommendations* section of the report, depending on content.

A description of the behavior(s) that prompted the referral for evaluation can be important background information. To understand under what conditions the subject exhibits certain behaviors can provide clues for clinical interpretation and recommendations for treatment. The fact that the subject becomes hostile or exhibits psychotic symptoms when using alcohol is valuable information. A good description of the behavior that prompted the referral can assist with determining the subject's insight and understanding about his or her situation. An account of specific behavior becomes particularly important when the referral question involves high-risk issues such as suicidal/homicidal ideation or attempts. That the subject almost bled to death from a self-inflicted wound is different from the case of an adolescent who voices a veiled intent to harm himself or herself if not allowed to stay out on a date until 1:00 a.m. Although both are important, they have different implications for psychological dynamics and intervention strategies. Statements about symptoms/behaviors that prompted the referral may repeat some of the referral question but should include detail beyond the brief *Reason for Referral*.

As indicated earlier, it is important to make clear in the report who is saying what about whom and under what conditions. This particularly holds true for the **Background Information** section of the report, given that much of its content is provided by collateral sources. Many reports read as if the writer is certain that what he or she has been told is fact when, in reality, it is second-hand information. When information comes from previous evaluations or other external sources, the sources should be cited. This could include the name of the person providing the information; for example, "Mrs. X, John Patient's mother, reported that John has difficulties relating to his father." If the mother said it, say so in the report. This will make it clear that the information provided is not the conclusion of the report writer but was obtained from a specific source. This also allows the reader an opportunity to question the credibility of the information in the context of who stated it, although if sources are of questionable credibility or are known to be dishonest, this should also be stated. Contradictory information should be reported as such. Not all information is necessarily valid, and this should be explained in the report when indicated. Such findings may contribute to interpretation, and some debate over fact versus fiction may result in improved understanding of the subject's psychological functioning.

BEHAVIORAL OBSERVATIONS

The purpose of the *Behavioral Observations* section is to provide the reader with as vivid a mental image as possible of the appearance and behaviors that the subject exhibited during the assessment. Through a comprehensive behavioral description, the reader should be able to have some idea of the motivation and attitudes of the subject during the evaluation. The manner in which the subject approaches the assessment process can provide valuable data about the cognitive and personality functioning of the subject and assist in determining whether or not the subject's performance should be interpreted in light of behavior (or lack thereof) that could significantly affect clinical conclusions. The subject whose anxiety level is so high that he or she has problems remaining on task will likely produce scores reflective of this. Behavioral descriptions such as "Subject kept focusing on different objects in the room" or "Subject was slow to respond to most tasks and stated, 'I really don't think I need to be doing this' " obviously have implications for the validity of test scores and will also provide clinical clues to the psychological functioning of the subject. The *Behavioral Observations* section is where that which the clinician sees, not infers, is described in behavioral terms and as straightforwardly as possible. The *Behavioral Observations* section is not the place to draw clinical inference such as "The patient was depressed during the entire evaluation." Concluding that the patient was depressed is content for the *Personality Functioning* section of the report. Describing the behaviors that may contribute to a later interpretation of depression is appropriate (e.g., "Poor eye contact," "Did not smile during the entire evaluation," and/or "Subject often sighed and stated 'I just haven't felt motivated to do anything lately' ").

Generally, we have found that one single-spaced paragraph covering about one-third to one-half of a page is sufficient for the *Behavioral Observations* section. We suggest that the report writer attempt to present the following information in this section. Obviously, not all of the information listed below would be included, and other relevant observations may better serve the evaluation.

1. Was the subject on time for the appointment? If late or absent, what excuse was given? Did the subject come alone or was the subject accompanied by someone? Who?
2. What was the general appearance of the subject? Height and weight?
3. Did the subject appear to have adequate personal hygiene?

4. How was the subject dressed? Loud clothes, lots of makeup, shirt on backwards, layers of clothing? Typical dress for age and cultural background?

5. When the purpose of the evaluation and limits of confidentiality were explained to the subject, how did the subject respond?

6. Was the subject friendly or hostile? Smile, laugh, or frown? (Provide behaviors which led to conclusions.)

7. Did the subject complete all test tasks asked of him or her? If not, why?

8. Were there indications of the motivation level of the subject? Did he or she give up easily? Did the subject eagerly approach test items or did he or she refuse or frequently state he or she was unable to perform the task? Did the subject seem to struggle or worry about his or her performance or seem to enjoy the process? Was prompting required? Did the subject do better when prompted?

9. Was the subject able to maintain focus on task or was he or she easily distracted? Describe.

10. Were there distractions or other testing conditions that could have an impact on the subject's performance?

11. Did the subject seem to have any problems expressing himself or herself or understanding what was stated by the examiner? Were there any indications of problems with vision or hearing (e.g., holding printed material close to the eyes, asking that verbally presented items be repeated)?

12. Did the subject exhibit unusual motor movement (e.g., tics, tremors, slowness, rapid movements, problems with balance or gate, asymmetry in appearance or movement)?

13. Did the subject respond differentially to different test items (e.g., on structured tasks such as the Wechsler IQ tests versus the unstructured tasks such as the Rorschach)?

14. During the clinical interview, did the subject talk openly or was he or she guarded about all or certain topics (e.g., the loss of a loved one or marital issues)?

15. Did the subject exhibit any bizarre or unusual behavior (to include verbal comments) during the evaluation?

16. Other observations.

An obvious concern is whether or not the subject arrives on time. Some subjects may not show up at all and another session has to be scheduled. Not arriving on time (or not being present) for the first scheduled appointment can have clinical implications and should be mentioned in the report. Describing the reason given by the subject or others for the subject not arriving on time or being absent at a previous scheduled session provides information about motivation and/or interest. Perhaps the subject was highly anxious or resistive or he or she was unable to adequately plan for a punctual arrival. Some subjects have valid excuses, but in our experience this is rare. Of course in hospitals or other institutional settings, this should be less of a problem, but still subjects in such settings can be late (e.g., slowly finishing a meal or being asleep at the time designated for the evaluation).

The appearance of the subject is important and should be described in this section. Issues of dress and hygiene as well as posture and other physical characteristics can be described (e.g., drooling or exhibits tremors). Behavioral manifestations of the side effects of medication can be important information for those subjects who have been prescribed psychotropic drugs and can be very helpful to physicians prescribing medication. Unusual motor movements such as difficulty with gate and the manifestation of tics should be noted. Asymmetry of body posture and movement can provide clues about possible neuropsychological problems.

Difficulties with sensory-perceptual functioning (seeing and hearing) during the evaluation should be noted in the *Behavioral Observations* section of the report. This information is vital to interpretation of results, because visual and auditory problems can affect test performance. Also, such difficulties can be a factor in psychological functioning (e.g., the impact of hearing loss on how a subject interprets what people say). We suggest clarifying any visual/hearing problems prior to the actual assessment for obvious reasons. Some subjects are reluctant to admit problems in these areas, and deficits are discovered during the course of the assessment. The subject who seems to have difficulty with details (e.g., Picture Completion of the WAIS-III) may actually have a visual problem. A statement to exemplify the preceding might be "Ms. Patient, though reporting that she has no problems seeing test items, would squint and hold items at arm's length."

Although addressed in terms of clinical relevance in other parts of the report, language usage is important. Did the subject exhibit problems with expressive speech and comprehend what was said to him or her? The behavior(s) that led the evaluator to conclude the subject was experiencing problems in these areas should be described. Did the subject have problems understanding simple instructions? Did the subject seem not to understand the vocabulary used? Problems with language usage should be described in the *Behavioral Observations* section without reference to cause or dynamics. Following sections of the report can address the reason for the deficits (i.e., in the *Intellectual and Cognitive Functioning* and/or the *Personality Functioning* sections of the report).

The level of cooperation the subject exhibits toward the evaluator is also reported. Was the subject hostile or suspicious? Did he or she refuse to participate in aspects of the evaluation or was he or she cooperative and friendly throughout? Did he or she smile at all? Describing what the subject does in behavioral terms cannot be overemphasized, and findings should be reported in detail. For example, a behavioral observation could read "Mr. Patient, at one point during the assessment, turned his head away from the examiner and stated, 'I am not going to do any more of this.' " By directly quoting the subject, little is lost to interpretation. Some subjects are overly compliant, and this too should be behaviorally described (e.g., "The subject frequently would ask 'Are my answers okay?' or 'Do you want me to tell you more?' "). Either way, the information is clinically significant.

Related to cooperation, but different, is the impact of motivation and interest on the behavioral output of the subject. The behavioral manifestations of the hypothetical construct "motivation" need to be described. To say the subject "lacked motivation" does not adequately convey to the reader the type and degree of the lack of motivation. A more appropriate statement would be, "The subject often looked around the room and frequently stated, 'Why do I have to take this crap?' " By contrast, some subjects seem eager to participate in the assessment process: "Mrs. Patient would reach for the next Rorschach Card without the examiner providing it to her." When prompting is necessary, this should be described in detail as well as how the subject responded to the prompting.

We have found, especially with adolescents and in institutional settings, that it is sometimes necessary to go beyond the standard test instructions. Subjects may require prompting and direction for a variety of reasons. When test instructions can be followed verbatim as written in manuals, this certainly is preferable and leads to better interpretive data. However, the reality is that some subjects require considerable prompting in order to perform adequately enough to provide data and information for interpretation. This is sometimes referred to as "testing the limits." When such methods are necessary, it is imperative that modifications be described in the report so interpretation can be made in light of these deviations from the standard administration process. Inferences should be given with recognition of limits imposed by altering the assessment process. Also the need to modify the assessment process often tells us something about the subject.

Some subjects have problems with concentration or attention and require redirection and refocusing. The degree to which this is necessary during the evaluation session should be noted. Often we have found, especially with hospitalized patients with severe mental illness, that frequent refocusing was necessary. We would describe this in our reports in a manner such as, "Mr. Patient had difficulty focusing on the task at hand. He frequently would seem to forget the task requested of him and would state 'They had no right to put me in here.' However, he was easily redirected to the assessment process without resistance." This observation has implications for the subject's capacity to function in treatment and also provides clinical clues about his or her cognitive focus and issues of attention. Such observations can also provide information about the subject's level of insight.

Observed behaviors are sometimes also mental status issues (e.g., "The patient frequently referred to himself as Jesus Christ"). The *Behavioral Observations* section is not the place for conclusions concerning mental status findings. Although it would be appropriate to include the previous statement in the *Behavioral Observations* section of the report, the conclusion that the subject is delusional, and any clinical interpretation of this delusion, is left for the *Personality Functioning* section. Psychological factors such as anxiety and depression should also be described in behavioral terms in the *Behavioral Observations* section. For example, the *Behavioral Observations* section might read "The subject was wringing his hands and reported excessive concern about his test performance." The psychological construct "anxiety" could be discussed in the *Personality Functioning* section with a statement something like "Assessment indicates that Mr. Patient experiences considerable anxiety which appears to be the result of. . . ." This is not to say that behavioral examples should not be used in sections of the report other than the *Behavioral Observations* section.

Aberrant and bizarre behaviors should be included in the *Behavioral Observations* section of the report and described in behavioral terms. Too frequently a report will simply state the subject exhibited "bizarre behavior." This is an inadequate description that does not provide the reader with a clear picture of the subject's behavior and could represent anything from the subject having his or her shirt on backwards to florid hallucinations. It is acceptable to use psychological constructs such as "hallucinations" as long as they are accompanied by vivid descriptive detail. For example, the report might read "The patient appeared to be hallucinating during the assessment. At one point he turned around, addressed what appeared to be an imaginary person, and stated 'I'll do it when I am damn ready.' This examiner asked him to whom he was talking and he stated. . . ." The same description should be given to behavior exhibited as a result of delusional thought. When aberrant behavior is cited in the *Behavioral Observations* section of the report, this should also be discussed in the results sections of the report. For example, to state "The subject was observed exhibiting rapid speech and jumping from topic to topic" without clinical interpretation would be inadequate, and the report writer would not be considering all the data available.

Most subjects will provide clues for clinical interpretation during the course of the assessment. For example, some subjects present suspiciousness or even paranoia during the evaluation. They believe that the assessment results will be used against them in some way. This may be a valid concern in some cases (e.g., court related evaluations), and, when such circumstances exist, the psychologist must interpret results in this context. Some questioning by the subject may be a matter of curiosity. However, the manner in which the subject interacts with the examiner is likely indicative of the way he or she relates to others and therefore tells us something about his or her interpersonal functioning.

Some observations will be stated as negative findings (i.e., not existing), "normal," or "typical." For example, there may be nothing unusual about the subject's appearance, and this would be stated in the report. Although this observation does not contribute to a particular problem, it tells the reader something about the subject during the interview and can lend to overall impressions. The absence of symptoms/signs is important to note.

The basic premise for the **Behavioral Observations** section of the report is to *describe what the subject says and does (or does not do or say, when relevant) in behavioral terms to the extent possible.* Psychologists, though supposed masters of human behavior, lack specificity in describing human behavior (Auger, 1974). To be behaviorally descriptive is not an easy task. Often it is easier and faster to describe behavior using summary statements, such as "Mr. Patient was reluctant to participate in the assessment" rather than putting the energy into developing a descriptive statement, such as "Mr. Patient stated 'I don't think this is necessary.' Then he put his head down on the examination table and said 'I am too tired to do this right now.' However, with prompting, he agreed to proceed with the assessment."

Obviously, not all the content presented here would necessarily be included in detail; this could make the **Behavioral Observations** section of the report much too lengthy. The clinician must choose the salient behavioral observations to include in the report, with the "heart" of the report remaining for the assessment results. Too much emphasis on observations that do not substantially contribute to psychological interpretation should be avoided. Observations help paint the overt or manifest level of the subject, while test results and dynamic interpretations may provide an understanding beyond the obvious. When these two components are integrated, useful comparisons can evolve for the results sections of the report. The subject who has been described in the **Behavioral Observations** section as "Ms. Patient was quiet and polite during the testing session and frequently thanked the examiner for 'taking your time to help me like this' " and then exhibits signs of significant hostility on projective assessment has provided information about his or her functioning on two different levels, which should make for interesting and useful interpretation of personality functioning. Again, this section is not the place for drawing clinical inference, although it will provide additional/supportive data from which results can be drawn.

Chapter 3

RESULTS SECTION: INTELLECTUAL AND COGNITIVE FUNCTIONING

Intellectual and cognitive factors can have a profound impact on psychological functioning and deserve separate attention in the psychological report. By "intellectual" we mean those areas of functioning measured by tests of intelligence; by "cognitive" we mean not what subjects think but how well they think (e.g., concretely, abstractly, efficiently, or with a memory impairment). The two are not separate. Cognitive processing is a component of intelligence. Neither cognitive nor intellectual functioning exist separately from personality, and one can have a significant effect on the other. Certainly cognitive impairment of organic origin can have a profound impact on personality. On the other hand, severely depressed persons have been known to have problems with concentration and memory, and depression can mimic a dementia. Psychologists are frequently called upon to assist in differential diagnosis between cognitive and personality factors. In order to do so, each area must be assessed and reported separately and then the effects of one on the other explained. The psychological report should include a section devoted to intellectual and cognitive functioning, and these results should be interpreted in light of the effects of personality and other factors (e.g., educational achievement and environmental factors).

Each test has its "organic look," and the experienced clinician can glean organic and intellectual indicators from personality tests (e.g., color naming and perseveration of content on the Rorschach) to include in this section. Mental status information obtained from the clinical interview may also be incorporated. Generally most clinicians employ a standardized test of intellectual functioning such as one of the Wechsler scales (Wechsler, 1974, 1981, 1989, & 1997) in their test batteries, for determining not only level of intellectual functioning, but also other cognitive functions. The Wechsler scales have been used to determine signs of brain damage and sometimes can be as useful in this respect as in determining level of intelligence or providing an IQ score. Often included in an *Intellectual and Cognitive Functioning* section are the results of some visuomotor test such as the Bender-Gestalt (Bender, 1938). We have found it helpful to also include a screening test for academic achievement level or functional literacy (e.g., reading and writing). These scores, when compared with intelligence test scores and other information, often provide useful data, especially for children and adolescents. No matter what tests are used, a structured format appropriately forces the psychologist to consider intellectual and cognitive functions across all test data and not just interpret a particular test to focus on a particular function. It would be a waste of information and neglectful to simply report an IQ level from a test of intelligence when subtest configuration, and even individual item analysis, might provide support for additional clinical inference.

Central nervous system functioning may be conceptualized on three different levels, and, depending on the experience and training of the clinician assessing the subject and writing the report, any one of these three levels could be incorporated into the report. The first level involves the development of this section from a general psychological assessment with no particular focus on specific neuropsychological issues. In this situation the referral question should not specifically relate to neuropsychological concerns, and the purpose of the report is generally about functional or nonorganic issues. However, given the potential interaction of organic and personality factors in determining human psychological functioning, screening for possible brain involvement is prudent. When screening produces negative results, a brief statement such as "Assessment revealed no indication of organic involvement" could suffice. However, when positive indicators do emerge, more explanation is warranted with the report detailing the suggested evidence.

When there is reason to suspect that neuropsychological factors may be involved but unlikely and secondary to the referral question (e.g., the history indicates that the subject had a minor head injury as an adolescent), then more focused assessment is needed and the report should reflect this focus to the extent necessary. This second level still represents a screening, and if the results indicate possible brain involvement, then referral for a complete neuropsychological evaluation seems warranted. Obviously, the content of the report should be reflective of this higher level of screening and provide more elaboration of supportive data.

The third level involves a comprehensive neuropsychological assessment, and the referral question specifically addresses a brain-behavior issue. This generally involves an extensive battery of tests focused on neuropsychological issues (e.g., Halstead-Reitan Neuropsychological Test Battery [Reitan & Wolfson, 1985] and Luria-Nebraska Neuropsychological Battery [Golden, Purisch & Hammeke, 1985]). For a psychological evaluation to incorporate this level of assessment into the report would likely alter the focus of the report such that it no longer is a general psychological assessment but a "Neuropsychological Assessment." It is not the intention of this text to include the findings of a comprehensive neuropsychological assessment in the structured format presented here. Although some overlap in these different levels exists, this text and the suggested format primarily address the first level described previously and those elements of intellectual and cognitive functioning that we feel should be included in a general psychological report when the referral issue is not thought to be specifically brain-behavior related.

Following are some content areas for inclusion in the *Intellectual and Cognitive Functioning* section of the report. Although consideration could be given to all the areas listed, it is unlikely that any one of these areas would be discussed in detail or all of the content areas included in the report of the general psychological evaluation. For this section, we suggest that, in most cases, two to three paragraphs covering two-thirds to a full page will be sufficient. Obviously, if intelligence subtest scores are reported, the length of this section could increase. We also suggest a summary paragraph at the end of this section providing the major finding (e.g., "On the test of intelligence, Mr. Patient scored within the Average Range, although educational and environmental factors may have negatively affected his performance. On a screening test for academic achievement, Mr. Patient scored on a third-grade level for reading and a second-grade level for spelling. On a test that screens for potential organic involvement, Mr. Patient performed adequately." Obviously, the suggestions to follow are subject to modification depending on the findings and the individual need of the referent. Specific questions that may be addressed in this section are:

1. How well was the subject oriented to time, person, place, and situation?
2. Did the subject exhibit any sensory-perceptual deficits?
3. Was the subject able to focus and maintain attention?
4. What was the subject's level of intelligence: IQ scores?
5. Were there factors that lowered or elevated the score from what is estimated to be the subject's true score (e.g., education, environment, motivation, testing conditions)?
6. Were there significant Verbal/Performance subtest differences? What is the interpretation of this?
7. Was there a significant intra-/inter-subtest scatter? Interpretation?
8. What was the subject's fund of general information? Vocabulary?
9. Was the subject's ability to perform abstractions intact?
10. Was the subject's visual organization functioning intact?
11. Were the subject's visuomotor functioning and motor speed adequate?
12. Was the subject's judgment impaired?
13. Was there any impairment in immediate, recent, and remote memory functioning?
14. Did the subject demonstrate any problems with language functioning, such as expression and comprehension?
15. What was the subject's level of academic achievement and literacy skills? How did the subject's level of academic achievement compare with the level of intellect?
16. Were there other observable or reported indications of possible neuropsychological involvement, such as physical asymmetry, tremors, blurred vision, headaches, or numbness?
17. Were there emotional issues that seem to be interfering with the subject's intellectual and cognitive abilities (e.g., depression, anxiety, or a thought disorder)?
18. Overall, what was the intelligence level of the subject and were there organic indicators?

ORIENTATION, SENSATION/PERCEPTION, AND COGNITIVE FOCUS

Orientation (Sensorium)

Essential to the subject's capacity to somewhat accurately perceive the world is the awareness of what is going on around him or her and to be oriented to who he or she is, where he or she is, and some idea of time (date). Also included in the subject's assessment of orientation is the capacity to understand the current situation or circumstance. This not only has implications for cognitive and personality functioning but also provides information concerning how well the subject is in touch with reality and can participate in the assessment. Sometimes poor orientation is the result of neuropsychological problems; other times it might be a consequence of psychosis. Whatever the interpretation, assessment of orientation or sensorium should be a component of the evaluation and a part of the report. Some clinicians may prefer to place orientation in the *Personality Functioning* section of the report as more of a personality construct or mental status issue. We have placed information on orientation in either section (and sometimes both) depending where we thought it would best fit.

Some report writers will state "Mr. Patient is oriented times four," meaning the subject is oriented in all four spheres (i.e., time, person, place, and situation). We prefer to state "The subject is oriented to time, person, place, and situation" for clarity. Of course, a positive finding could be stated, for example, as "Subject was oriented to time, person, and place but did not seem to understand why he was in the hospital." When such positive findings exist, more elaboration may be required to help with interpretation. In many cases, there will be no need to elaborate because the subject will likely be well oriented and a simple statement as "The subject was oriented to time, person, place, and situation" should suffice. Although in some settings, such as in psychiatric hospitals, where persons may manifest significant problems with orientation, this may not be the case and more elaboration would be appropriate. Persons who do not know who they are are generally grossly impaired from either an organic or a personality perspective. Also persons who are disoriented to place are generally fairly impaired. However, not knowing the date is more common and, in many cases, may not be indicative of psychopathology. The subject who is unaware of his or her current circumstance may be significantly cognitively impaired or may be attempting to deny or avoid the reality of the situation. In any case, some exploration in an attempt to discover why he or she is not oriented may be helpful to interpretative information when positive findings do exist.

Sensation/Perception

To what extent the subject is able to sense and perceive accurately his or her environment is important to the psychological evaluation for several reasons. Obviously problems with vision or hearing can have a significant impact on test performance and the extent to which deficits affect performance should be described in the report. Psychologists do not traditionally formally evaluate these functions, although through observation during testing, it frequently becomes clear whether or not the subject experiences problems in these areas. Also, sensory-perceptual deficits can provide clues concerning possible organic involvement as well as problems of a psychological origin. Visual and auditory deficits of a peripheral nature (e.g., farsightedness, hearing loss) may require mention in the *Intellectual and Cognitive Functioning* section with the suggestion in the *Recommendations* section that the subject have a visual/audiological examination. Olfactory, tactile, and gustatory problems are less likely to be discovered in the course of the general psychological assessment, but should be mentioned in the report if found. Numbness, blurred vision, or loss of the sense of smell reported by the subject, discovered through the course of testing, or indicated in collateral sources of information, could have serious implications for central nervous system functioning as well as test performance. When subjects exhibit such deficits in the course of the evaluation session, this probably should have been described in the *Behavioral Observations* section of the report and results reported in the *Intellectual and Cognitive Functioning* section.

However, most frequently such deficits are not apparent during the course of testing, and negative findings can simply be stated in a relatively brief concise sentence such as "Mr. Patient did not exhibit signs of sensory-perceptual deficits." When positive signs are discovered then more elaboration may be necessary to describe the observed deficit(s). The general psychological report is not the place to draw medical conclusions, although some situations may be clear and straightforward and can be explained in the report to the extent necessary and appropriate to the level of training of the clinical psychologist. For example, if the subject has reported that he or she is blind in one eye or is "hard of hearing," this can certainly be mentioned; but to go into an extended explanation of the physiology behind the deficit is not appropriate for this report and beyond the training of the psychologist. Pointing out that a subject reported blurred vision is not conclusive of anything except that the subject reported blurred vision, although this could provide support for the possible rejection or acceptance of hypotheses about brain functioning. Also, sensory-perceptual deficits can have a significant effect on personality functioning; to not hear well can contribute to paranoia, and such findings could be integrated into the *Personality Functioning* section of the report.

Cognitive Focus (Concentration and Attention)

Although some subjects demonstrate clear problems with concentration and attention, others demonstrate more subtle problems in this area which, to one degree or another, affect their cognitive functioning. Problems with cognitive focus can be the result of any one of several etiologies (e.g., psychosis, anxiety, or depression). Drugs and medical problems may also produce such symptoms. Central nervous system (CNS) dysfunction may be implied. Determining the exact etiology, though important, is often not possible at the time of the writing of the report, if ever. Such is frequently the case with attention deficit problems. Just providing an awareness that the problem exists, can be helpful to treating clinicians and others involved with the subject. Recommendation for more specialized evaluation, both medical and psychological, can be provided in the *Recommendations* section of the report.

When problems with cognitive focus, concentration, and attention appear to have functional (psychological) etiology, the impairment can be mentioned briefly in this section with expansion, in terms of the dynamics, in the *Personality Functioning* section of the report. However, when organic (central nervous system) causes cannot be ruled out, elaboration in the *Intellectual and Cognitive Functioning* section of the report is recommended. Also, it is certainly appropriate to discuss problems with cognitive focus in both sections of the report as they relate to both CNS and personality functioning. Statements concerning problems with cognitive focus are generally brief in the general psychological report and may simply state "Evaluation indicated that Mr. Patient appears to be having problems with focusing on task and assessment revealed attention deficits." The recommendations section might state "Mr. X appeared to be experiencing problems with cognitive focus and attention, and referral for neuropsychological assessment to assist in determining the extent and possible etiology of this problem is recommended."

INTELLECTUAL FUNCTIONING

Frequently, the *Intellectual and Cognitive Functioning* section is primarily focused on the intellectual functioning of the subject. Evaluation of intellectual ability is one of the areas of expertise that psychologists generally can offer to assessment. Over 40 years ago, research indicated that the majority of referring psychiatrists felt that an IQ score should be included in a psychological report (Tallent & Reiss, 1959a). Although in some cases it may not be possible or appropriate to give a full evaluation of intelligence, we recommend that some idea of the subject's intellect be given and that these findings be included in the psychological report. Some clinicians may choose to use "short forms" or brief intelligence tests (e.g., Wechsler Abbreviated Scale of Intelligence; The Psychological Corporation, 1999). When these have been validated and are appropriate for the purpose of the evaluation, they may provide useful information to the reader. In such cases, the report writer should state that the results represent an estimate and make it clear that a "short form" was employed. For example, the report might read, "On a short form of an individually administered test of intelligence, Ms. Patient scored an estimated IQ within the Average Range." The *Sources of Information* section should cite the specific test. When a formal assessment of intelligence is not completed, an estimate based on the evaluator's knowledge of the correlation of intellectual functioning with other assessment results, review of collateral information such as school records, and the assessor's observation of the subject's functioning during the evaluation should be reported. When no formal testing is given, the report might read, "Through review of school records and psychological test data, as well as the subject's observed abilities during the session, it is estimated that Ms. Patient is functioning within the Average Range of intelligence."

When an intelligence test such as one of the Wechsler scales is completed, Subtest Scale Scores may be presented along with the IQ scores for the Verbal Subtests, Performance Subtests, and the Overall IQ, or Full Scale IQ as presented previously. Under these scores, depending on the tests given, the individual subtest scores can be presented as follows:

On the test of intelligence, Ms. Patient scored within the Average Range with a Verbal IQ of 98, a Performance IQ of 101, and a Full Scale IQ of 99. Subtest Scale Scores are presented below:

Verbal		**Performance**	
Information	14	Picture Completion	12
Similarities	12	Picture Arrangement	11
Vocabulary	15	Block Design	9
Arithmetic	11	Digit Symbol	11
Comprehension	12	Matrix Reasoning	9
Digit Span	14		

After an overall statement of the general level of intelligence of the subject is given, along with aggregated subtest scores, such as the Verbal and Performance composite scores of the Wechsler scales, interpretation of subtest scatter can be presented. This can start with a statement about any significant difference between composite scores and then go into an interpretation of subtest scores. Subtests can then be reported individually or can be grouped into constructs. For example, the Wechsler scales of intelligence have developed norms for aggregating subtests into different factors, for example, developing a single INDEX score from different subtests purported to measure similar things. When the subject scores poorly only on those tasks involving visuomotor coordination, deficit performance is reported. This finding is likely more powerful than single subtest interpretation, although such is not always the case.

Frequently the overall IQ score is not reflective of the subject's potential level of intelligence and must be interpreted in light of subtest scatter. For example, we have encountered results of intelligence testing (Wechsler scales) with a relatively low Verbal IQ. Examination of subtest scatter reveals significantly low scores on the Vocabulary and Information subtests relevant to all other subtest performance. Recognizing that these two subtest scores can be affected by environmental and educational factors, it is plausible that the subject's score was lowered by these factors and that the true level of intellect is somewhat higher. This inference can be supported by other data such as poor academic achievement scores and/or poor school performance. It is reasonable to conclude that if the subject had acquired a better vocabulary and fund of general information, he or she may have scored higher on the test of intelligence. The addition of such "qualifiers" to the results of intelligence testing depicts a more accurate representation of the subject's true potential which can have grave implications for expectations and treatment. This also indicates that the report writer has taken a common-sense integrative approach to assessment and just not "cookbook" or "test-and-tell" report writing as discussed earlier. It is imperative to keep in mind the audience of the report, and if there is reason to believe that subtest scores would be interpreted erroneously or taken out of context, then perhaps the report writer might consider not including the scores. However, generally these scores, in the hands of a competent and ethical clinician, can be very helpful for diagnostic and treatment purposes.

It is also important to keep in mind that when reporting test scores, we are doing just that - reporting test scores. To do so without interpretative integration of factors that likely affected these test scores could provide an erroneous conclusion about the subject. At the same time, intelligence test scores are likely more objective than other forms of psychological testing, such as projective assessment, where interpretation has less statistical backing. With intelligence testing we prefer to provide the reader with the test scores and add information that alters the interpretation of those scores, explaining how different factors impact the subject's scores. In this manner the reader can see that the subject scored one way but that, given other factors, the true level of functioning is likely different than that reflected by the actual test score.

One of the major problems encountered with intelligence testing is that of "baseline"; that is, what was the subject's level of intelligence at some point in time before the current assessment? If the subject is being tested for the first time, objective baseline data may not be available. However, sometimes previous scores are available making comparison relatively easy (if one has confidence in the accuracy of the scores). Collateral information may provide a useful estimate of baseline intellectual functioning for comparison with current functioning. For example, if the subject was employed as a nuclear physicist 3 years ago and currently scores an IQ of 82, something is likely wrong and the score may represent a decrement from a previous level of functioning. Certainly such comparisons and other information concerning "baselines" are important to include in the report. However, caution is in order; decrements or increases in IQ scores do not necessarily mean the subject has deteriorated or suddenly become smarter. We have experienced differences of 20 IQ points or more as a result of such factors as motivation, effects of medication, and severe depression and anxiety. All test interpretation must be made in the context of the total person.

ACADEMIC ACHIEVEMENT

We have found it helpful to include in this section, along with findings of intelligence testing and other cognitive functioning, information about the subject's academic achievement. This is particularly relevant to school-age children and adolescents. Consequently, we generally include a brief screening test of academic achievement in our battery such as the Wide Range Achievement Test-3 (Wilkinson, 1993) or the Wechsler Individual Achievement Test (The Psychological Corporation, 1992). We feel these instruments have limitations, but if cited and used as screening tests to be interpreted cautiously, they can be very helpful in obtaining a general idea of literacy skills. They also can be useful for comparison with IQ scores to obtain some sense of over- and underachievement. One frequent finding is the adolescent who performs poorly on an academic achievement test and makes low grades but scores well above average on the intelligence tests. The challenge for the clinician is to find out why this youth is not functioning up to potential. A statement in the report might read, "Ms. Patient, on a standardized screening test of academic achievement, scored at a third-grade level for reading, although she scored above average on the test of intelligence. Psychological factors appear to be interfering with her ability to learn and reach her potential." We also generally provide scores from academic achievement tests but qualify them as representative of a "screening." A specialized psychoeducational assessment would be needed to provide more conclusive results in this area and may be an appropriate recommendation.

LANGUAGE FUNCTIONING

Statements about the subject's ability to express himself or herself verbally and understand what is said is relevant to cognitive functioning. Language usage, to include both positive and negative findings, should be noted. If there is no evidence to indicate that the subject is experiencing any problems in this area, a simple statement such as "Mr. Patient did not exhibit indications of problems with expressive or receptive language functioning" will usually suffice. If problems are discovered, these should be noted with as clear a description of the deficit as possible. For example, "Ms. Patient scored well below average, and below her other subtest scores, on verbal subtests of the test of intelligence." Such information may be tied into other findings such as a poor reading level on an academic achievement test with a statement such as "Her poor verbal performance is supported by a low score on the reading portion of a screening test of academic achievement." For the general psychological report, it is not expected that the report writer will have the expertise to provide a detailed analysis of specific forms of language difficulties such as different types of dysphasia. It would certainly be appropriate to describe strengths and weaknesses in this area but not to draw any conclusion about the complexities of language function. One or two sentences about language will generally suffice. Those clinicians with specific expertise in this area may want to elaborate further. Some subjects may be from another culture and English, for them, may be a second language. When a language difference is of concern, it is suggested that the report writer consult with a person of the same culture who speaks the same language as the subject, if possible.

OTHER SPECIFIC
COGNITIVE FUNCTIONS

Strengths and weaknesses in specific cognitive functions can be discussed in the *Intellectual and Cognitive Functioning* section of the report. Data from a variety of sources can be used in determining deficits and strengths. Discussion of such factors might have already been accomplished when addressing the results of intelligence testing and the relative performance on different subtests. For example, the subject may perform well above average, relative to other subtests, on the Similarities Subtest of one of the Wechsler scales of intelligence, and this could be cited when discussing subtest scatter. Or data from multiple sources could point to strengths and weaknesses (e.g., performing poorly on the Block Design subtest of one of the Wechsler scales and also performing poorly on the Bender-Gestalt; Bender, 1938). Both point to possible problems with similar functions. The number and type of possible cognitive factors are many, and it is not the purpose of this text to review them all; nor is it the purpose of the general psychological evaluation to cover all the complex possibilities for cognitive functioning. Below are presented some of the more common cognitive indicators that we have found helpful to include in the general psychological report.

Visuomotor Functioning

Along with a test of intelligence, most general psychological test batteries include a separate test of visuomotor functioning. This is often referred to as a test of perceptual-motor functioning. Generally, these are brief paper-and-pencil tasks which require the subject to copy geometric shapes of some kind. Common examples include the Bender-Gestalt (Bender, 1938), the Hooper Visual Organization Test (Hooper, 1983), and the Memory-for-Designs Test (Kendall, 1962). Subtests of the intelligence test can also be used to determine visuomotor organization ability (e.g., Block Design and Object Assembly of the Wechsler scales). Other tasks that involve visual organization functioning, such as drawings, can provide supportive data. There are many instruments, and components of other instruments, that can evaluate this function. Positive findings on these tests are generally fairly telling and point to possible brain involvement. However, these instruments tend to produce a considerable number of false negatives concerning overall brain damage. That is why it is important to also look at other functions, such as language.

Visuomotor measures can provide a lot of information which can be teased out from the data. First, the clinician must discern if the subject understands the task (comprehension). Second, the subject must sense the stimulus, that is, he or she must see it. To do this, visual functioning comes into play at the receptor level (in the eye). The third component is perception; that is, whether the brain sees it accurately (sent to and organized appropriately on the visual cortex). The fourth aspect is whether the brain can then integrate the visual input with its motor component. The final question is whether peripheral functioning is intact (e.g., reception of nerve impulses in the muscle of the arm or hand). The report writer may not be able to determine at which of these levels impairment exists, but he or she should be able to determine if the subject can see the stimulus correctly or if tremors are so pronounced that they are likely causing subaverage performance on the task. When reporting the existence of errors or poor performance on tests of visuomotor organization, it is important for the report writer to describe the type of aberration. Certainly, the subject who provides a clear reproduction of the stimulus but rotates the image may have a related but different problem than the subject who destroys the gestalt of the stimulus.

Drawings of any type can add to projective interpretation of personality functioning. Some clinicians are quite good at interpreting designs that are representative of psychological dynamics. Certainly figures that are expansive and haphazardly placed on a piece of paper can be reflective of different personality attributes than those of the subject who draws very small reproductions that are all placed against the left-hand border of the paper. For those clinicians who make such interpretations, findings should be included in the *Personality Functioning* section of the report.

When assessment of visuomotor function produces negative results, a simple statement such as "Subject performed adequately on a separate test of visuomotor organization" is generally sufficient. Positive findings on tests of visuomotor organization, unless explained away (e.g., due to tremors as a result of withdrawal from alcohol), deserve description. For example, "Mr. Patient exhibited deficits on a test of visuomotor integration to include perseveration and destruction of the gestalt of the designs." If other tests support this position, this can also be mentioned. In the ***Recommendations*** section a referral to a clinician with expertise in neurological and/or neuropsychological assessment would be made.

Abstractness-Concreteness

The capacity to perform abstract operations has been associated with good brain function, while concreteness has often been associated with impaired functioning. The ability to abstract is a component of intellectual and cognitive functioning, and we suggest that it be represented in the psychological report. Verbal abstracting may be impaired, while nonverbal abstracting remains intact. The former is sometimes measured by verbal generalizations such as on the Similarities Subtest of the WAIS-III, while nonverbal abstractions might be measured by tasks that involve application of a general principal to a visual-association task, such as the Wisconsin Card Sort (Heaton et al., 1993). The general psychological assessment may not include the idea of nonverbal abstracting; in those cases, reporting the results of measures of verbal abstracting capacity is generally acceptable. Along with formal psychometric measures, the subject's use of language during the evaluation session may contribute to the assessment of verbal abstracting capacity. When subjects perform well on abstract tasks, a one-sentence statement in the report concerning this issue will suffice and might state, "Mr. X's ability to perform verbal abstractions seemed unimpaired." When subjects perform poorly, elaboration concerning the actual performance of the subject becomes important. It is also important to keep in mind that different cultures use abstractions differently, and these differences should be factored into interpretation.

Calculating

Problems with calculating (e.g., relative poor performance on the Arithmetic Subtest of the WAIS-III) may or may not be indicative of central nervous system dysfunction. Anxiety and depression can interfere with the ability to concentrate to the degree needed to perform accurately even relatively simple math without the aid of paper and pencil. This is a difficult differential to assess. Sometimes it may be necessary for the report writer to state that the subject also exhibited signs of emotional states that could contribute to poor performance. Also, the distinction between written and verbally performed calculations may point to different brain origin (Levin & Spiers, 1985). For the general psychological report it is sufficient to simply state that the subject either did well or did not do well when performing the specific type of math used (e.g., "Mr. Patient, on a task involving verbally presented mental math, without aid of paper and pencil, performed well above average"). If the report writer has the knowledge and ability to differentiate between types of calculating dysfunctions, then certainly this can be presented. Remember it is acceptable for the report writer to describe what he or she sees without drawing a conclusion beyond the scope of his or her expertise.

Memory

A review of the *DSM-IV Text Revision* (American Psychiatric Association, 2000) provides one with an appreciation for the importance of memory in cognitive dysfunction. For example, to give a diagnosis of any of the dementias requires that there be an impairment in memory functioning as part of the clinical picture. Memory can be an unreliable measure of central nervous system dysfunction because it is significantly affected by psychological factors (Lezak, 1983). One need only review the experimental literature on forgetting to understand the importance of psychological factors in memory functioning. Problems with storage and retrieval are often evident in nonorganic disorders such as depression and anxiety. The interference of psychological states with consolidation and storage of material is well known. Differential diagnosis between organic and psychological factors affecting memory is exemplified by the term *pseudodementia* and represents a clinical challenge well suited to the expertise of the clinical psychologist.

We almost always include an assessment of memory functioning in our psychological reports. Three areas of memory functioning should be included: (a) immediate, (b) recent, and (c) long-term or remote. It is important to have clear definitions for each of these, and clinicians tend to define them in different ways. For the purpose of this text, immediate memory will be defined as that part of memory which allows us to recall material immediately after the stimulus has been removed. Recent memory involves the recall or recognition of material in which there is a period of time between the stimulus withdrawal and recall. Generally, this period of time may be relatively short (e.g., a few hours) or substantially longer (e.g., several days). Shorter periods of time between stimulus and recall that are not immediate should probably be specifically defined (e.g., "After a 20-minute delay Mr. Patient was able to recall. . . ."). Long-term or remote memory involves the recall of material that has been stored for an extended period of time. Time between stimulus presentation and recall may be several weeks to several years. If the event to be remembered occurred yesterday, it would be referred to as recent memory; however, if the event took place a year ago, this falls into the long-term or remote area. There are no discrete cutoffs when generic terms are used, and we assume that the reader will have a general idea of the difference between the three types of memory by virtue of their labels. If specific tests are employed to assess memory, the type of memory measured should be described in the text's manuals, and this information can be presented in the report.

Probably the most important of the three types of memories is recent. It is relatively unusual for individuals, unless severely cognitively impaired, to exhibit significant difficulty in immediate memory, although if one works in a geriatric setting or assesses persons in confused or delirious states, immediate memory may be commonly impaired. Obviously, deficits in immediate memory can have devastating effects. The more common clinical finding in most traditional assessment batteries (other than no memory impairment) is impairment in recent memory. This form of memory deficit generally points to the lack of consolidation of new material and can have a significant negative impact on functioning. To not remember the events in one's childhood or younger years may not have such a grave outcome as forgetting that one turned the stove on one-half hour ago. However, the importance attached to different memories must be taken in context (e.g., to not remember that one is married could be a problem).

The extent to which memory impairment is assessed and reported is dependent on the experience of the evaluating psychologist and the purpose of the report. When results indicate that the origin of the memory problem is psychological as opposed to organic then a statement concerning the impact of psychological functioning on memory is also reported in the *Personality Functioning* section of the report. Statements about memory are usually included along with statements about problems in cognitive focus, concentration, and attention, given the interactive nature of these psychological functions. In the general psychological evaluation, a relatively brief statement concerning the three types of memories will suffice and often only require one line, such as "Mrs. Patient exhibited no indication of problems with immediate, recent, or remote memory." Positive findings, as usual, will require more elaboration. Some clinicians may attribute conclusions about memory directly to test results (e.g., "On measures of memory functioning, Mrs. Patient exhibited no indication of impairment in immediate, recent, or remote memories"). However, as with most clinical inferences, we believe conclusions are the result of a composite of information which includes much more than just a test score.

LOCALIZATION AND DEGREE OF IMPAIRMENT

As with other findings, the extent to which the report writer comments on localization of impairment is partially dependent on his or her expertise. We suggest that localization is usually not reported in the general psychological evaluation, and if results indicate possible organic involvement, referral to a clinician with advanced knowledge in this area is recommended. However, evidence for localization may be so compelling that to not mention it would be an inappropriate omission. For example, the subject may have been in a car accident with left-hemisphere involvement demonstrated by Magnetic Resonance Imaging, and psychological testing reveals a significant decrement in language functioning when compared with baseline data acquired prior to the accident. In this case, a statement about the effects of left-hemisphere involvement is likely warranted. Another example is when tests reveal significant intellectual deficits, including memory deterioration, in an 80-year-old subject. Obviously, the possibility of dementia is present. In both these cases, while the evidence may be pointed, it is not conclusive, although hypotheses for further assessment can be presented.

Describing the degree of impairment in a useful way for the reader can be a difficult task. Some evaluators make a highly subjective statement by labeling the impairment as *mild, moderate,* or *severe.* We suggest that such terms be used sparingly, if at all. More appropriately would be to mention the presence of signs of impairment and, to the extent possible, describe the assessment results that led to that conclusion. For example, the report might state, "On a test of visuomotor integration, Mr. Patient produced several rotations, perseverations, and destructions of gestalt. This is indicative of possible central nervous system dysfunction." When the data are definitive and the examiner/report writer has the knowledge and experience to draw more specific conclusions about the localization and degree of possible organic impairment, then this information should be included in the psychological report.

REPORTING QUESTIONABLE FINDINGS

In general psychological practice, opinion can vary greatly concerning whether or not to report organic findings when the evidence is not that compelling. A relatively longstanding concern has been that to label a patient as "organic" is the "kiss of death" and will mean a poor prognosis with little, if any, intervention. Also, there exists the belief that persons who are considered to be "brain damaged" will be discriminated against in different ways. These possibilities can certainly be valid and therefore, it is very important that we be conservative in giving such labels. However, to ignore positive signs could have an extremely negative impact on the subject and even result in death. These concerns must be weighed in the best interest of the subject.

The report writer should also exercise caution in differentiating between organic and psychological causes for positive findings. As most experienced clinicians realize, psychological symptoms can mimic organic symptoms and vice versa. Also, it is important to recognize that although psychological symptoms may not be the direct cause of organic involvement, they may be secondary to it. For example, a subject may become depressed due to recognition of his or her organic impairment. We believe that it is a rare situation when either psychological or organic origin stands completely alone; most subjects present a much more complex interactive picture.

CONCLUSION: INTELLECTUAL
AND COGNITIVE FUNCTIONING

There are many areas of cognitive and intellectual functioning; those discussed previously should not be considered exhaustive. A broad-range approach to intellectual and cognitive functioning is recommended. Which functions to assess and report will be dependent on the expertise of the psychologist and the purpose of the report. Although the *Intellectual and Cognitive Functioning* section of the report primarily focuses on intelligence and cognitive factors, clues to the subject's personality functioning may also be discovered in the course of assessment in this area.

Chapter 4

RESULTS SECTION: PERSONALITY FUNCTIONING

INTRODUCTION

Writing the *Personality Functioning* section often poses the most difficulty - and usually the most anxiety - for the student and the relatively inexperienced psychologist. The problem stems in part from the difficulty of abstracting and integrating the whole issue of personality dynamics and structure. The ease with which the clinician can conceptualize personality and developmental issues, see their relevance to current mood, affect, and behavior, and apply these to a diagnostic nosology will dictate the comfort level with the actual write up of the personality assessment. Accordingly, it is imperative that the clinician have a firm grounding in personality theory, developmental psychology, psychopathology, and learning theory. Equally important, of course, is the clinician's familiarity with and expertise in the personality instruments utilized as part of the testing battery. Because most referral sources are asking questions relevant to personality functioning, a major focus on personality features seems appropriate. The *Personality Functioning* section is often the heart of the psychological report and probably should predominate in terms of length and content.

The personality instruments utilized play a role in the problems in writing the *Personality Functioning* section. Unlike the recounting of the person's background or the empirical (hard) data arrived at by intelligence testing, the examiner has to integrate relatively subjective (soft) data into an understandable and helpful format. It is this dual difficulty - the relatively subjective results from personality instruments coupled with the overall need to integrate these results into a cohesive personality description - that often intimidates the developing clinician.

As mentioned earlier, the characteristic report of a novice writer involves a long, detailed background information section, coupled with one or two sparse paragraphs of actual personality assessment. Although, as indicated in the previous sections, a background information section is of strong importance in the writing of a good report, it is the interpretation and integration of assessment results that constitute the main contribution that a psychologist can bring to the assessment of a human being in the clinical setting. To rely on background information to provide the bulk of the report is to underutilize the very tests that allow psychologists to make such a unique contribution. Another sign of the inexperienced psychologist is the cookbook recitation of personality test findings mentioned earlier. The cookbook approach simply lists personality features without any attempt to merge them into the facts of the subject's individual life. The growth in popularity of computer administered tests and computerized interpretation makes the cookbook style more common today. Personality features are often couched in tentative and probabilistic language such as "Individuals with similar profiles may be likely to. . . ." or "This person may occasionally have experienced. . . ." This type of language is often so broad and vacuous as to be virtually meaningless in the applied clinical setting. The writer must exert some clinical judgment rather than simply operate as a computer in spitting out actuarial statements. Thus, to say "Authority struggles are indicated" is made more potent if superimposed on the person's history (e.g., "Authority struggles - such as currently experienced with his employer - are reflected by the projective data and are probably related to his father's stern discipline during his childhood"). The examiner thus uses the data to generate a hypothesis and then integrates the hypothesis into a meaningful clinical observation consistent with the background information that has been gathered. This moves from an abstract generalization to useful clinical findings that have direct application to therapeutic intervention.

Another variant of the cookbook approach is the rote test-by-test-result style without any attempt at theoretical integration. As indicated before, this is a serious mistake and significantly weakens the value of the report. This is particularly true of the *Personality Functioning* section. A major drawback of this approach is that such a format is entirely meaningless to any reader not familiar with the test instruments. A more general fault is that it tends to produce a rambling and disjointed format. Tests are enumerated with results (often in meaningless codes) appended to them. Contradictions in findings are incompletely reconciled or, more frequently, ignored and not commented upon by the examiner. The reader is left with an impressive, technical-appearing compendium of unrelated facts that have little utility. It is this very avoidance of application to clinical reality that attracts the neophyte writer. It is far easier to recite results than pull together facts into a meaningful whole. The most extreme example of this type of flawed report was seen several years ago by the authors when reading a report that listed the response to each card of the Thematic Apperception Test (TAT; Murray, 1943) without comments or interpretation as to its application to the patient. Because there was no attempt at interpretation, there was no opportunity to integrate the TAT findings with other test data and the patient's personal history. What was left was a 12-page report that was very technical in appearance, but of essentially no value to the reader.

The typical personality assessment battery is likely to contain one of several objective personality inventories such as the MMPI-2 (Hathaway & McKinley, 1989), the Personality Assessment Inventory (Morey, 1992), the Beck Depression Inventory (Beck, 1978), the Millon Clinical Multiaxial Inventory-III (Millon, 1994), or other measurements. It is important to remember that responses to such tests are generally based upon the patient's self-report and represent the patient's view of himself or herself. Although, as in the case of the MMPI-2, the information can be viewed actuarially, personality inventories represent only one plane of personality assessment. A deeper plane relies on projective testing, most notably the Rorschach and TAT. At least theoretically, projective personality instruments allow access to the preconscious and unconscious levels of personality functioning and are not reliant upon an individual's self-report and hence self-perception.

All levels and types of personality testing can be usefully woven into the *Personality Functioning* section if several principles are kept in mind. The first principle is to avoid single-sign analysis of data. Single-sign analysis involves making an interpretation about the personality functioning of a subject from one positive finding or indication in the test data. Abstracting from several different indications of the same interpretation is recommended. As each individual test instrument is scored and interpreted, cumulative signs will begin to emerge. For instance, on the MMPI-2 certain scales will be elevated, certain indicators will appear on the interpretation of TAT cards, certain features of projective drawings will become apparent, and certain content or quantitative analysis of the Rorschach will point toward certain interpretations. Thus, the results can be abstracted into possible interpretative statements. Single-sign analysis is to be avoided in that it is highly unlikely that a single feature of any one test will accurately portray a person's overall personality functioning. Multiple findings need to be integrated and then combined into general interpretive statements if they are seen consistently through the test results. Then, and only then, can clinical hypotheses about the subject be generated. Once the clinical hypotheses are generated they can be turned into specific statements regarding the subject's personality functioning and general psychological perspective. Finally, after abstracting, integrating, and applying the data to a person's unique personal situation, the report is written so as to convey the information in a meaningful, appropriate format to the reader.

As stated before, the reader's "need to know," level of training, and overall professional sophistication should be taken into account in writing the report. Thus, a report to an attorney would be organized and written differently from one to a psychiatrist or to a school teacher. This is particularly relevant for reporting results regarding personality functioning, which can be quite sensitive and confidential.

THEORETICAL FORMULATION

The theoretical perspective from which a report is written may vary from report writer to report writer and will be dependent upon the training, experience, and knowledge of that writer. Whether the writer has a behavioral, interpersonal, or psychodynamic background, the important requirement is that the writer has a sufficient command of personality theory and psychopathology to utilize these concepts in the conceptual development of the subject's personality. A singular theoretical perspective will be quite limiting. We suggest that the report writer be somewhat eclectic and, as a minimum, have some under-standing of ego psychology as well as cognitive-behavioral, interper-sonal, learning, and psychodynamic theories.

This leads to a question of the *Personality Functioning* section's theoretical orientation. Historically, report writers have favored a psy-chodynamic approach to conceptualizing the report. This probably has been based on the preponderance of graduate schools with ego psy-chology/psychodynamic orientations as well as the nature and struc-ture of some psychological tests. With the advent of cognitive-behavioral therapy, solution-focused therapy, various brief therapy models, and the overarching influence of managed care, fewer and fewer clinicians are practicing psychodynamic therapy. However, it is our anecdotal impression that many therapists today are practicing a cognitive-behavioral (or other brief, focused therapy) style without totally abandoning a conceptual view of the patient's dynamics. Thus, inclusion of psychodynamic issues is still of value and still welcomed by referents. However, integrating other current therapy concepts into such a framework can be of value particularly if the referent employs similar theoretical approaches in practice. Integrating the two theoreti-cal stances is not as difficult as one might imagine. For example, it might be said: "Mr. X has a low self-concept and has introjected a negative image of himself. This relates to his father's berating, sarcas-tic style of discipline and competitive domination of his son. He has internalized anger at his father, and the anger has caused a chronically depressed affect. Negative self-statements and automatic thoughts, centering on failure and his inability to be perfect, maintain this self-image."

Another example would be of a passive individual who is unable to address an all-powerful parental figure in a confrontive and healthy fashion. Such an individual would often use the psychodynamic mecha-nism of displacement to externalize the anger at another (uninvolved) individual. A cognitive-behavioral therapist would be interested in examining how attributional statements toward the "all-powerful" fig-ure maintain the patient's passive stance and reinforce the schema of helplessness.

The previous edition of this book emphasized a psychodynamic bias toward test interpretation and report writing. Although our ap-proach supports the position that there is a subconscious and that persons do feel emotions of which they are not consciously aware, we recognize that not all reports need incorporate such dynamic constructs. An approach that emphasizes more overt concepts, such as cognitive-behavioral theory or a behavioral perspective, is certainly acceptable and in some settings may be the preferred point of view. For example, helping the report reader understand a patient's cognitive schema, dichotomous thinking, or the nature of automatic, maladaptive thoughts are all possible and valuable components of the well written report.

Still, personality is not unidimensional; we advocate the use of a "layered" or "levels" theoretical perspective. An example of a layer or level system that we have found to be particularly helpful incorporates many of the concepts developed by Timothy Leary in his text entitled *Interpersonal Diagnosis of Personality* (Leary, 1957). He presents a multilevel system depicting five levels of personality. The primary advantage of Leary's system is that the levels correspond to different psychological tests, and consequently test results are readily applied to his system. We have borrowed from Dr. Leary in a simplified form as suggested by Rabin (1981). Instead of five levels, Rabin uses three: (a) the way others see us, (b) the way we see ourselves, and (c) those thoughts and feelings which are distant from awareness. Here preconscious and subconscious have been lumped under one broad category, although they could be broken down into different levels, treating the preconscious and subconscious as two distinct levels, as does Leary. Such a distinction is certainly acceptable in psychological report writing.

We are suggesting that the ***Personality Functioning*** section of the report conceptually integrate these three levels of personality to include (a) the overt behavior of the subject (the way others see us), (b) the subject's self-evaluation (the way we see ourselves), and (c) the underlying "distant thoughts and feelings" (preconscious and subconscious) which are often responsible for the first two levels or manifest behaviors. Different personality concepts and variables can be discussed in terms of these different levels. This provides the reader with considerable knowledge as to the general awareness and insight of the subject (and others) concerning his or her psychological state. It is very important to keep in mind that the different levels of the personality are not necessarily discrete entities. In fact, they may overlap considerably. In Leary's (1957) framework, good mental health is defined as a sufficient degree of congruence between the levels. Thus, we see ourselves as others see us, and underlying needs and tensions are not so out of line with these overt levels as to cause problems.

To illustrate this framework for personality structure, one could almost use any personality variable or interpersonal factor. For example, someone who feels that he or she is emotionally appropriate (Level II) may be perceived by others as paranoid and hostile (Level I), while on an underlying level (Level III) this individual may be significantly depressed.

Rabin (1981) also describes another level that falls between Levels I (others' perception of the subject) and II (how the subject sees himself/herself). This level, which he refers to as Level IA, is the subject's perception as to how others view him or her. It is completely plausible that one's perception as to how others view him or her may be different from the subject's self-perception and also different from the way others actually do view the subject. For example, the subject may have a self-perception as direct and confronting, but feels others view him or her as rather meek and passive, while in reality others may view him or her as angry. This Level IA is similar to insight.

We believe it is advisable to divide the ***Personality Functioning*** section into subsections: (a) ***Emotional***, (b) ***Intrapsychic***, and (c) ***Interpersonal***. The three areas are certainly not mutually exclusive and many blend into one another. However, all are felt to be representative of important dimensions in personality. When viewed together, these three components can paint a vivid picture of an individual's psychological functioning. No separate heading is necessary for emotional, intrapsychic, and interpersonal functioning. They are included under the ***Personality Functioning*** section.

EMOTIONAL FACTORS

The emotional state refers to the most overt level of psychological life (i.e., the manifest mood and affect and the behaviors driven by these states). This section contains components similar to those of a Mental Status Examination but provides the latitude to integrate aspects of other levels of personality if appropriate and explain manifest behavior in more detail. No separate heading is required and we suggest this subsection be a single paragraph in length and the first paragraph of the ***Personality Functioning*** section. Specific content that may be discussed in this subsection include the following:

1. Is the subject oriented to time, person, place, and situation? (This may have already been addressed in the ***Intellectual/Cognitive Functioning*** section or may be in both places.)
2. What was the affective state of the subject: appropriate, inappropriate, flat, constricted, wide range, labile, blocking, or hypomanic?
3. Did the subject report any significant emotional stress or manifest symptoms of severe emotional distress, such as agitation or anxiety reaction?
4. What was the prevailing mood of the subject: sadness, hostility, or paranoia? Did the subject's mood vary?
5. Did the subject exhibit looseness of association, tangential thinking, pressured speech, or flight of ideas? Were there indications of idiosyncratic speech, deviant verbalizations, or other odd statements?
6. Did the subject exhibit delusions, hallucinations, feelings of depersonalization, or other signs of possible loss of reality contact?
7. Did projective testing or other indicators reveal that the subject may decompensate under stress? Are there indications that the subject has decompensated in the past or has become extremely depressed or manic?
8. Were there other behavioral manifestations (e.g., withdrawal, histrionics, fearfulness)?
9. What is the extent of the subject's ability to control affect, such as anger?
10. Did the subject report feeling depressed/anxious? Problems with loss of appetite, sleep disturbance, or loss of interest in sexual activity? Psychomotor retardation?
11. Has the subject exhibited suicidal/homicidal ideation in the past or present? To what extent is such a finding present, and what is the nature of this ideation?
12. What other overt behaviors/emotions did the subject exhibit?

The issues of sensorium (orientation as to time, person, place, and situation) was discussed earlier as it related to intellectual and cognitive results. As indicated, issues of sensorium may be appropriate for the *Emotional* subsection of the report if they add to the reader's visual imagery of the manifest nature of the personality. If cognitive (neuropsychological) factors are felt to be etiological, then sensorium may be briefly stated in this section with more description provided in the *Intellectual and Cognitive Functioning* section. However, if psychological factors are felt to be involved, more clarification is indicated. Obviously, the underlying reasons for these psychological factors may be discussed in other areas of the *Personality Functioning* section. For example, if a subject believes he or she is an Apostle of Christ and has been placed on Earth to save the world by setting fires to any place the voice of God commands (e.g., a government building), then the relevance of orientation to not only personality functioning, but also diagnosis and treatment, becomes obvious.

Indications of a thought disorder should also be included. These entail such disturbances of thinking as looseness of associations, tangential thought, deviant verbalizations, abstract thinking, and odd or peculiar statements. Also, this section should address the subject's speech pattern (i.e., "Does the subject present with normal, slow, or a rapid rate of speech?"). Is the subject's speech pressured or hesitant? While these constructs likely should have been described in the *Behavioral Observations* section, their relevance to personality functioning should be described in the *Emotional* subsection.

In the *Emotional* subsection, the prevalent mood and affect are discussed in terms of strength, duration, congruence with one another, and suitability/adaptability. Some clarification of the difference between mood and affect may be useful. A helpful analogy is as follows: Mood *is to* affect as climate *is to* weather. This analogy serves to differentiate between a long- and short-term emotional state and helps delineate the two concepts. It is also important to know if the affect (weather) is incongruent or in variance to the overall mood (climate). Just as a hot day in the Arctic is notable, so would be an elevated or giddy affect in an overall depressed individual or in the context of a situation where most people would be distressed. In addition, a person presenting with a flat or constricted affect after discovering he or she had won a million-dollar lottery may tell us something about the level of depression this individual is experiencing.

Obviously, other dimensions of affect can be relevant, as well as the incongruence of mood with the presenting situation. Also noteworthy is the breadth of affect and its implications for underlying emotional states. Some individuals may be extremely constricted in their ability to display their emotions, while others exhibit an extremely wide range, to the point where they may present quite differently on two different occasions. This is often the case with bipolar disorders and, at times, schizophrenia. Certainly, flexibility and adaptability of affect are indicators of good emotional functioning. However, extreme deviations from the average can be representative of severe psychopathology.

Also included should be an assessment of the level of the subjective distress. A statement such as "Assessment reveals that Mr. X is experiencing a significantly high level of emotional stress" or "On an objective personality inventory, he is reporting severe psychological discomfort" could suffice. Another acceptable statement could include the following: "Mr. X reports little felt emotional distress. However, psychological testing reveals that he is masking his emotions at this time." Data from objective personality inventories and mental status observation may be useful in the completion of this subsection. An individual will often exhibit profiles that are indicative of his or her felt emotional distress. Other instruments, particularly projectives, seem to be more precise in determining underlying feelings of personality structure; for the most part, those results are probably best discussed in the intrapsychic component of the *Personality Functioning* section of the report.

Although somewhat different, the prevailing mood is related to the emotional stress level of an individual. The level of stress generally indicates the felt emotional distress of the individual. However, many individuals present to others on an overt level (Level I) in a manner different from that which they experience themselves (Level II). For example, the hypomanic patient may view himself or herself as experiencing no difficulty. The clinician obviously sees something different. Sometimes the patient will present with considerable hostility and paranoia and genuinely believe that there is no problem. A patient's mood may be extremely variable, changing during the course of the evaluative session and/or over days or weeks. Such variation should be noted in the report.

Issues of impulse control and affective modulation should also be addressed. When anger is expressed more directly, and/or testing reveals that the subject is experiencing difficulties monitoring emotions and behaviors, the writer needs to thoroughly address the "acting-out" potential of the individual. This can include homicidal/suicidal ideation or overt tendencies. Whether or not the person is likely to successfully modulate these impulses and has the capacity to sublimate or rechannel emotions are factors to be carefully considered. Although the clinical psychologist cannot predict future behavior, psychological and environmental factors as well as the history of the individual could play a role in "acting-out" and should be addressed in the report. The ability to deal with one's emotions effectively, as well as what factors may lead to an inappropriate expression of emotions, should receive mention. The role of alcohol and substance abuse may be included here. However, oftentimes these factors are considered more representative of intrapsychic forces (i.e., the alcohol breaking down repression as an ego defense resulting in the manifestation of anger).

Bizarre behaviors of different types should be noted here as well as in the *Behavioral Observations* section of the report. The difference, indicated earlier, is that the *Behavioral Observations* section should operationalize concepts to the extent possible. Although such operationalizing is also appropriate for the *Personality Functioning* section, clinical inference can be drawn in the latter. For example, in the *Emotional* subsection of the *Personality Functioning* section, one might state that the subject "experiences auditory hallucinations," while the *Behavioral Observations* section reports that "The subject looked to one side and said that the voices kept distracting him." In the *Personality Functioning* section, clinical terminology and constructs can be utilized (e.g., depression, anxiety, psychosis). Indications of delusions, hallucinations, feelings of depersonalization, or other signs of reality contact problems are obviously extremely important. A description of the delusion/hallucination should also be given where possible. A patient who believes his brain is being eaten from the inside by an electronic signal presents with significantly different dynamics from a patient who has a delusion that his wife might be involved with another man. The same is true of hallucinations. The content of hallucinations can provide significant data from which to draw inferences and clinical conclusions. However, underlying dynamics are often left for the *Intrapsychic* component of the *Personality Functioning* section rather than the *Emotional* subsection.

Feelings of depersonalization can present on a continuum and may be appropriate content for this section. A subject may state, "I do not feel like myself." Others may report that they have had "out-of-body" experiences or other more pathological indicators. The combination of language usage and cognition can provide valuable data. Illogical sentence sequencing, looseness of association, and/or flight of ideas are obviously appropriate for this part of the psychological report. Other overt manifestations (e.g., histrionics, withdrawing, and apprehension) may also be noted.

Psychological testing may reveal that when under stress and/or under the influence of drugs or alcohol the subject may decompensate into psychosis or exhibit other underlying manifestations of problems. Some subjects may mask their depression through histrionics or hypomania. Although the manner in which the ego structure changes to produce such manifestations is left primarily for the *Intrapsychic* subsection of the *Personality Functioning* section, mention of such possible decompensation/masking may be appropriate for the *Emotional* component of the *Personality Functioning* section of the report. Statements such as "Although Mr. X exhibited no indications of overt psychosis, assessment reveals that when stressed, he may decompensate and his reality testing may become tenuous" or "Mr. X, while reporting no significant symptoms of distress on the surface, may, when stressed, exhibit significant depression" can be appropriately utilized to lead into the area of intrapsychic dynamics.

Overt reports of feelings of depression, hopelessness, loss of appetite, sleep disturbance, mania, or other indications of affective disturbance can be reported in this section. As briefly mentioned earlier, suicidal behavior may be a manifestation of poor affective modulation and impulse control difficulty. Due to the grave consequences of such manifest behavior, this issue should be thoroughly and prominently addressed. Suicidal ideation and/or related behavior should be described within this initial component of the *Personality Functioning* section. Negative findings should also be reported. The recentness of suicidal thoughts, as well as behaviors, should be noted, and it is important to provide some description of the patient's thoughts concerning this subject. To state that the subject has had "vague suicidal ideations" is too cursory. What does the word "vague" mean? To state that the patient reports that he has thought about harming himself three times in the last month, but has never had a plan or seriously wanted to die, provides a much better clinical picture of the subject's potential for such behavior.

The same is true of homicidal ideation. Basically, it is important to cover this area in terms of whether or not such ideation is present or has been present, to what extent it is present, and the nature of the ideation. Latent self-destructive indications (as in the case of suicide by continual drug abuse or placing oneself in extremely hazardous situations) is important material and can reveal future potential. This information should be included in the *Intrapsychic* portion of the *Personality Functioning* section as well as in the *Summary and Recommendations* section.

INTRAPSYCHIC FACTORS

The second of the three parts of the *Personality Functioning* section of the psychological report deals with the intrapsychic structure of the personality. The American Psychiatric Association (1980) defines intrapsychic as "that which takes place within the psyche or mind" (p. 53). We define intrapsychic somewhat by exclusion in that it is that part of the personality which is not emotional nor interpersonal, although some overlap between dimensions exists. Much of the *emotional* component refers to overt manifestations of personality such as affect, mood, thought organization, and subjective stress; the *interpersonal* subsection deals with that which goes on between persons. The *Intrapsychic* subsection refers to that which underlies the manifest behaviors of both the emotional and interpersonal areas of personality.

A subject may exhibit manifest indications of depression (i.e., flat affect and problems with concentration on an emotional level) and be withdrawn and alienated on an interpersonal level. These overt personality concepts are often symptomatic of underlying dynamics. The *Intrapsychic* subsection presents these dynamics and is probably the most challenging in terms of conceptualizing personality. Although some seasoned clinical psychologists may be able to draw conclusions about the intrapsychic structure of the personality after observing overt behavior, intrapsychic structure and its complexities are not obvious to the observing clinician without making inferences or interpreting psychological tests, particularly projective instruments.

The term intrapsychic almost implies that forces within the personality underlie what one sees on the surface. Certainly the analyst would agree with this approach. Other theoretical positions also support this "onion" or "layer" conceptualization. Peeling back the surface layer of the onion exposes what is underneath. Cognitive-behavioral theorists may regard this as the level of "automatic thoughts" which are not immediately in the awareness of the patient. Ego psychology also emphasizes such a position as well as conflict approaches. It is the *Intrapsychic* subsection of the *Personality Functioning* section that requires the integration of the elements of the personality into a conceptual whole, which can explain the overt behavior. The information provided in the *Intrapsychic* subsection is extremely valuable to the psychotherapists in planning treatment.

The approach we employ for the intrapsychic functioning of the personality could be described as psychodynamic emphasizing ego psychology with an integration of behavioral concepts. Other approaches to personality conceptualization are certainly appropriate and, in some settings, preferred. For example, in a school environment, emphasis on a "here-and-now" behavioral approach may prove more beneficial to teachers and students than a psychodynamic approach. Even within a psychodynamic framework, we support the integration of behavior concepts as a means of making personality dynamics more practical for application. Also, a psychodynamic approach does not necessarily exclude behavioral dynamics. On the contrary, behavioral concepts such as reinforcement, punishment, escape, and avoidance are inherent in most psychodynamics. For example, is not repression a form of escape from unwanted or unacceptable affect such as anxiety or anger and probably maintained via negative reinforcement? Often subjects repress their anger as a means of escaping the uncomfortable anxiety (tension) experienced when they fear their own hostile impulses. Reaction-formation and repression as ego defenses may also provide relief from such tension and consequently are negatively reinforced and anxiety-reducing mechanisms (Sullivan, 1947).

Questions related to intrapsychic functioning for inclusion in the *Personality Functioning* section of the psychological report include:

1. What are the ego defenses utilized, and how do they manifest themselves in behavioral terms?
2. Is there underlying anger/hostility? What is its probable etiology?
3. Does the subject internalize or externalize feelings?
4. Does the subject deal with such feelings directly in a passive-aggressive fashion, or through displacement?
5. Are there underlying tensions and conflicts?
6. Are there manifest indications of intrapsychic conflicts and tensions, such as hallucinations and delusions?
7. What is the subject's self-image? Are there issues of identity? Are there latent self-destructive indications?
8. What is the level of the subject's insight into his or her difficulties?
9. What other intrapsychic psychological forces exist (e.g., obsessions, compulsions, and guilt)?

Ego Defenses and Underlying Affect

The *Intrapsychic* subsection of the *Personality Functioning* section can include a description of the ego defenses employed and how they are utilized. Ego defenses have been commonly referred to as the "defense mechanisms." The word mechanism denotes something mechanical, such as a working part in a hydraulic system. As we push down in one place, another place comes up. Dynamics of ego defenses operate in much the same fashion. If we repress more anger, we are likely to see more displacement. If we use more denial of our own role in our difficulties, we are likely to project more. The ego defenses do something: They handle uncomfortable feelings and try, in some manner, to reduce the anxiety associated with such feelings. It is beyond the scope of this work to explore defense mechanisms in detail, but the reader is urged to develop a working familiarity with the principles of defensive operations.

Sometimes testing will reveal underlying emotional states that are extremely basic to the personality. These emotional states may manifest themselves on the surface as anxiety, anger, depression, agitation, or through a serious mental illness producing looseness of associations, delusions, or even hallucinations. One example of the workings of underlying emotional states can be demonstrated by the behavior of some active alcoholics. When the alcoholic drinks, the effect of alcohol tends to disinhibit underlying affect (often anger). The alcoholic, under this condition of weakened ego control (i.e., ego defenses break down) allows the anger to receive expression (this is not always the case; some persons seem to be affected by alcohol in the opposite manner by withdrawing). When sober, the alcoholic often feels guilt about the anger he or she has exhibited, although this anger generally remains repressed. Consequently, tension again builds and the alcoholic may drink to release such tension.

The direction and targets of the emotions should also be mentioned in the report. By "direction" we mean either the externalization or internalization of the emotion, and by "target" we mean that to which the emotion/tension is directed. The "target" may be almost any person, place, or thing. However, feelings such as underlying anger most often seem to be directed toward other persons. This brings in an interpersonal element, and for this reason, the details of such findings would more appropriately be placed in the *Interpersonal* subsection of the report. However, statements such as "Mr. X denies his anger relevant to his perceived inadequacies and tends to displace blame onto others in his life" is certainly appropriate for the *Intrapsychic* subsection. The *Interpersonal* subsection can follow up with a more thorough explanation.

Whether or not subjects externalize or internalize their affect/emotion has grave implications, not only for treatment, but also for establishing expectations about overt behavior. If a subject tends to externalize under certain conditions and internalize under other conditions, this can provide clues concerning self- or other-destructive behavior. Recommendations for monitoring such behavior or reporting "Anger is likely to receive expression when the patient is under stress" is appropriate content for both the *Intrapsychic* and *Emotional* subsections. However, if the resulting behavior is most often overt, it is recommended that this be mentioned in the *Emotional* subsection with follow-up explanation of the underlying psychodynamics in the *Intrapsychic* subsection.

Conflicts

Another area for inclusion in the *Intrapsychic* subsection is that involving the internal conflicts of the subject. Conflicts can create considerable anxiety as the personality feels pulled in different directions. To not address this issue, particularly relevant to psychotherapy, would be a serious injustice to the report and the subject.

Different psychological factors can cause intrapsychic conflict. Latent identity concerns, trust issues, or conflicts over the expression of unacceptable feelings can create considerable anxiety as the ego attempts to deny or repress feelings and displacing or projecting defenses develop. The anxiety created by the conflict is the important dynamic variable that can be measured by psychological testing and observation. It is conceivable that conflicts may be minimal and create little anxiety. The extent to which the conflict creates anxiety is dependent upon a complex integration of psychological factors that probably would never be completely understood. From our assessment process we should be able to gain some insight into the degree to which a particular conflict causes an individual psychological discomfort. As an example, when presenting information on intrapsychic conflicts, the psychological report might read as follows:

> Assessment reveals that Mr. X is experiencing considerable paranoia and resulting problems with trust. This appears to be the result of underlying feelings of inadequacy which create considerable anxiety for him. He denies these feelings and does not accept responsibility for the role he plays in his difficulties, projecting blame outwardly onto others. This is exemplified in his tendency to see himself as the victim of those whom he believes are against him and to blame others for his shortcomings. This behavior alienates others and consequently confirms his underlying feelings about himself as one who is not accepted and. . . .

In the preceding example, the conflict is explained rather than just simply listing the major defenses involved. Conflict should be explained in terms of (a) what manifest behaviors/emotions are a result of the conflict (a high degree of anxiety), (b) how the patient views himself or herself, as a result of the conflict (being persecuted, people out to get him or her), and (c) the underlying conflict and dynamics (e.g., denial of the problem and the manner in which the ego defenses deal with the conflict). An inappropriate and cursory way of reporting the same information would be as follows:

> The assessment reveals that Mr. X is experiencing a considerable degree of paranoia. He feels inadequate and anxious. He uses the defenses of denial and projection. He feels alienated and not accepted by others and. . . .

Although the latter statement gives the basic facts, there is not coherent integration of these facts. It does not tell the reader how these personality findings go together to describe the intrapsychic dynamics and how they function. It does not tell the reader why the patient does what he does. Although it is true that many experienced clinicians could assimilate this material and draw the proper conclusions, this should be done for the reader by the report writer. If isolated pieces of data are given, the reader is left with his or her own projections to decide how the different pieces fit together.

Intrapsychic conflicts can also be conceptionalized from a behavioral perspective, such as approach-avoidance and similar paradigms. Conflicts of this nature are sometimes found in subjects with avoidant personality features. Although these individuals desire to be close to other people, conflicting feelings (e.g., trust versus mistrust) can result in withdrawal. An example of this approach follows:

> Assessment indicates that Mr. X is experiencing significant anxiety concerning trust issues. Although he desires to be closer to other people and express his feelings more openly, problems with trust inhibit this process. He fears that if he were to express what he actually thinks and feels he would become vulnerable to exploitation and criticism. His avoidance serves to reduce his anxiety resulting in negative reinforcement for having withdrawn. This approach-avoidance conflict creates. . . .

Overt Manifestation of Intrapsychic Issues

As mentioned previously, manifest behaviors relevant to psychological functioning are generally reported within the *Emotional* component of the *Personality Functioning* section. This is true for behavior usually indicative of psychopathology such as delusions, hallucinations, looseness of associations, or thought blockage. Such severe manifestations are in service to the ego and help the subject lower anxiety, although usually only temporarily and often in a maladaptive and repetitive manner. In other words, the personality "has a purpose" in manifesting such behaviors, and these behaviors can have very clear and interpretive meaning. For example, it doesn't take a great deal of knowledge to recognize that the person who hears a voice telling him to kill himself is probably a suicidal individual who is unable to admit his own self-destructive impulses and projects these feelings onto an external "voice."

Behavioral manifestations, along with their interpretations, should be described in the psychological report to the extent possible. By explaining such behavior, important concepts, which otherwise might be unrecognized, are given to the reader. Even illusions or akoasms (e.g., hearing a voice calling one's name), can have important interpretive meaning and deserve mention. A subject who hears his mother's voice calling his name can have a different meaning from the subject who hears an unidentified voice. The same is true for visual hallucinations, as well as tactile, gustatory, or olfactory phenomena. The personality dynamics of a subject who has olfactory hallucinations of burnt flesh may be quite different from those of the subject who smells a woman's perfume.

Intrapsychic Self-Perception and Identity

The issue of self-image (whether one feels good or bad about himself or herself) can be addressed in the *Intrapsychic* subsection of the psychological report. The term self-image is a relatively vague concept and often is used as a catch-all category. Too often a report may read "Mr. X has a poor self-image and lacks confidence." This gives the reader little information. A poor self-image about what? Lacking in confidence about what? Is the poor self-image due to being overweight or is it a result of the subject feeling intellectually inferior?

Does the subject lack confidence in performing his or her job or in dealing with the opposite sex? To merely address self-image as a trait construct is too general and leaves the reader with too many unanswered questions. Giving the reader some insight into why the subject either feels good or bad about himself or herself provides valuable information to therapists, teachers, and others. A statement that pinpoints the self-image issues can provide content for the *Recommendations* section of the psychological report.

Self-image, self-perception, or self-concept are not strictly intrapsychic entities. Many clinicians believe that self-image is a product of our interaction with others and consequently is an interpersonal phenomenon. It is probably true that many of our perceptions about ourselves result from how we believe others view us. From a developmental perspective, it is not too difficult to see the results of abusive alcoholic parents upon the self-image of some children. The child's negative sense of self, although probably lost to conscious awareness, is often incorporated and drives behavioral patterns that reinforce this poor self-image. Such persons often become abusive and alcoholic or extremely dependent persons who feel no one wants them. Consequently, it might appear that self-image can be very much an interpersonal issue. Although this is true, we believe self-image also has much intrapsychic significance. There are underlying factors which seem to be etiological, and consequently we believe comments relevant to self-image belong in the *Intrapsychic* subsection of the report. However, what goes on between people to contribute to the self-image may be integrated into the *Interpersonal* subsection.

Projection can play a role in one's self-concept. Often our projections are influenced by the way in which we believe others see us. It is possible to believe that others are viewing us differently from what is actually the case, and others' perceptions of us may be distorted by their own projective needs. Consequently, self-image becomes much more than just how we see ourselves; it becomes how we see ourselves in relation to how others see us and how such distortion interferes with our own and others' perceptions. For example, it is not unusual for testing to show that an adolescent feels he or she is not meeting parental expectations relevant to academic performance. This specific self-perception is important to note in the report. It also may be discovered that the parents have a different expectation about grades than the subject believes they do. Comparison with a normative standard may reveal that both the parents and child are distorting not only each other's expectations about grades, but also the generally accepted standards.

Closely associated with self-image is the idea of identity. Identification as a defense and identity (who I am), though related, may mean very different things. Identification with the aggressor means the subject may incorporate values, characteristics, or traits of another person as a means of warding off anxiety or threat from that individual. This could play a primary role in the forming of one's "identity" or self-image. Although we believe an analytical approach to identity and self-image can be useful, we also support a more here-and-now interpretation for psychological report writing and suggest, where appropriate, there be an integration of the two perspectives. For example, it is certainly feasible for test data to reveal that the subject may experience underlying conflict relevant to identification (as identifying with a significant other with whom there are feelings of both love and anger). However, at the same time, it is realistic to conclude that current unsuccessful encounters with other persons can affect the subject's sense of identity.

There are specific problems to address when making statements about identity or self-image. Some reports include only issues related to a negative self-image. Certainly, positive self-image concepts are just as relevant and provide the reader with knowledge of areas of psychic functioning that can be tapped and reinforced. Some subjects may have an overinflated sense of self-worth, as is often seen in manic persons, which will require description in the report. One must exercise caution in making statements of identity, particularly in the sexual area. Such statements should be validated in some manner with manifest behavior unless evidence from the assessment seems overwhelmingly conclusive. Issues of identity are not limited to individuals or individual traits. Group identification is possible, as well as identification with a profession or other significant aspect of life.

Sometimes test data reveal self-destructive signs related to poor self-image. The subject may or may not have conscious awareness of these feelings. It is important to describe such dynamics in detail, when they exist, and attempt to give the reader some idea of potential for self-destructiveness based on manifest or latent content. This may need to be integrated with overt behavioral indications (e.g., recent suicidal ideations/behavior, level of depression, or sense of hopelessness).

Insight

The question as to the presence and extent of insight should be addressed in the psychological report. Some subjects may be considered to be less than insightful in that they have developed delusional thoughts about their situations. Others may rationalize or develop other invalid conclusions relevant to themselves. On the other hand, patients may exhibit significant insight, but appear unable to make positive changes in their lives. Insight indicates that the subject has some sense of self-responsibility for his or her psychological state and difficulties. Insight on both an emotional and cognitive level is desirable and represents a significant asset.

We cannot expect subjects to be totally accurate in their self-perceptions. In addition, one can become philosophical and ask, "What is true in reality?" As discussed earlier, how we see ourselves may be totally different from the way others see us, and who is to judge which is right or wrong? However, we do measure our behavior by certain standards, and subjective norms are very often a basis for comparison even in psychological reports. Whatever we determine to be the patient's level of insight or lack thereof deserves mention. Elucidation of degree and type of insight is warranted in the report.

The importance of operationalizing and specifying cannot be overemphasized when dealing with insight. To just say the subject has "no insight" or "considerable insight" is insufficient and leaves the reader hanging. No insight about what? Considerable insight into what? An example of a statement that provides some description relevant to the question of insight follows:

> Mr. X appears to exhibit little insight into the psychological dynamics described previously. He does not recognize the extent of his anger nor his passive-aggressive means of dealing with his anger and may continue his self-defeating patterns despite overtly wanting to change.

This informs the reader that the subject does not possess much insight and how this relates to his overt behavior. In our format, issues of insight have been placed toward the end of the *Intrapsychic* part of the *Personality Functioning* section. Insight into one's intrapsychic processes is probably most relevant to a person's ability to control, modify, and adjust behavior from an internal perspective. Insight can also relate to an emotional state as well as to interpersonal behavior, and it would not be inappropriate if statements about insight that referred to several different personality variables were to be included.

It would be impossible to describe all the different psychological dynamics, traits, defenses, and other variables that could be used in formulating intrapsychic functioning. We have attempted to briefly present a few of these concepts here. The choice of what to include or not to include in terms of personality functioning is dependent upon the referral question, the subject's psychological state, and the theoretical perspective and knowledge base of the report writer. No matter what personality factors are present, it is important to keep in mind the audience and its level of understanding concerning intrapsychic processes. Intrapsychic dynamics can lend themselves well to an intellectual exercise and provide for a stage where psychologists can show what they know (and sometimes what they don't know). However, if what we write is beyond the expertise of our reader, it has little practical value.

INTERPERSONAL FUNCTIONING

H. S. Sullivan (1947) believed that personality development is the result of interpersonal experience and can be conceptualized only within that context. In other words, what goes on between people is the crux of personality development. He further believed that much of personality is maintained via interpersonal behavior. Interpersonal behavior can be viewed as a here-and-now phenomenon or can be related to past experience. Although there is certainly some merit in Dr. Sullivan's position, to present personality as a totally interpersonal phenomenon may not represent the overall clinical picture of an individual and may not be in the best interest of the psychological report or the subject. As stated previously, intrapsychic or emotional personality factors are often related to interpersonal phenomena; this can be elaborated upon in the *Interpersonal* part of the *Personality Functioning* section.

In any case, we are suggesting an *Interpersonal* component to the report. The description of interpersonal behavior can be a single paragraph in the *Personality Functioning* section and requires no separate label. We suggest that this subsection follow the *Intrapsychic* subsection. Specific content for this section, like that of other sections of the report, may vary. Questions the writer might entertain in the development of this section of the psychological report include, but are not limited to, the following:

1. Is the subject's posture toward other persons interpersonally passive, active, hostile, and/or dependent? Is the subject an independent individual? Are there issues of autonomy versus dependency?
2. Does the subject believe that he or she fits into society and/or is a part of a social group? Does he or she feel alienated, rebellious, or antiauthoritarian?
3. What is the subject's psychological position within the family structure? Are there family systems issues? Does he or she feel alienated from family? Are there particular family members for whom the subject has unresolved feelings?
4. Does the subject exhibit schizoid/avoidant features or extroversion and social comfort?
5. Are there issues of unmet affectional or dependency needs?
6. Is the subject attention seeking or manipulative?
7. What is the subject's social learning approach? What kind of behaviors does the subject emit that may evoke rejection and subsequent alienation? Are there secondary gains (e.g., attention and manipulation)?
8. What is the patient's level of social skills?
9. Are trust issues evident? How do such trust issues manifest? Are there abandonment issues or rejection concerns?
10. Do interpersonal conflicts exist (e.g., marital, familial, extrafamilial)? How do these conflicts manifest themselves?
11. What other interpersonal issues are relevant?

Interpersonally Passive-Active/Hostile-Dependent

We recommend that the *Interpersonal* subsection of the report include a statement about a "passive-active" dimension for the subject in relation to other people. Although such a personality dimension may seem to relate well to an interpersonal approach-avoidance paradigm, another related meaning exists: that is, one in which a subject represses or internalizes feelings about people rather than externally expressing feelings. For example, if the subject is angry, instead of confronting the object (significant other) of the aggression with anger, he or she may just back off. We believe it is a rare situation when things just stop there. Often a passive posture results in a displacing of aggression. Hence, the term "passive-aggressive." Probably most people, if not all, have some element of passive-aggressiveness in their makeup. Such behavior can be very destructive if for no other reason than it tends to frustrate those persons around the subject and is self-defeating.

We recommend the combining of modifiers relative to interpersonal dimensions. For example, an extremely dependent person can also be passive. In the text of the report this can be referred to as "passive-dependent." This means that in interpersonal encounters the subject is both passive and dependent. Also, it is certainly possible that an individual can be active and independent or passive and independent (though the latter case is less likely). There are additional possibilities, including the subject who is passive-dependent *and* passive-aggressive. In reporting such combinations of interpersonal dynamics, it is important to explain the parameters surrounding the behavior. This is more or less operationalizing the dynamics involved. For example, if we say a person is passive-aggressive, it is important to elaborate. We might state:

> Mr. X, when angry with his wife, tends not to express his feelings toward her directly. Instead, he internalizes his feelings, taking a passive stance, and indirectly expresses his anger through other behaviors which are frustrating to her. Such behaviors include his chronic lateness and unwillingness to participate in social activities, which she desires. Such behavior is self-defeating for Mr. X, in that it continues his maladaptive pattern of behavior in a repetitious manner, never addressing his anger nor his conflicts with his wife. She in turn becomes very frustrated and tends to withdraw from him. Such behavior does allow Mr. X to externalize his anger, although indirectly, relieving some of his depression.

One can clearly see the difference between the preceding and an inadequate statement such as: "Mr. X tends to relate in a passive-aggressive fashion." The former statement appropriately tells the reader much more and paints a clearer picture of what the subject's life is like relevant to the dynamics. It also allows for a clearer perspective as to what can be done about the situation in treatment.

Hostility resulting from conflictual interpersonal relationships is an important characteristic of personality that often deserves mention in the report. If one accepts the premise that too much dependency breeds hostility, the term hostile-dependent takes on important meaning. Hostile-dependent relationships often have a passive-aggressive component. A clear statement of such dynamics in the psychological report can be very useful to clinicians and other individuals concerned with the case. Remember, it is imperative to indicate to whom the hostility is directed, how it manifests itself, and how and upon whom the subject is dependent.

Issues of Autonomy (Independence)

Although a hostile-dependent relationship refers to an interpersonal process where one component (dependence) can lead to another (hostility), autonomy is more of a developmental process - a struggle between one's striving for independence and one's dependency needs. Obviously, such processes are part of normal development, but they can be pathological when they become distorted, extreme, or fixated.

Clinicians tend to associate such conflicts with adolescence. However, struggles for autonomy continue into adult life and probably throughout the lifespan. Autonomous development can be an extremely anxiety-producing process that may be acted out in different ways. For example, the psychological report may state "The patient is dealing with issues of autonomy versus dependency and his rebellious behavior is a result of this struggle. Through his rebellious manner, the patient exerts his independence." Such a statement is certainly valid content for the psychological report.

Autonomy versus dependency struggles may also represent a "deeper" or more serious level of pathology. For example, schizophrenic patients may be so enmeshed within the family structure that they are unable to separate or "individualize." An overincorporating mother (and/or a family system that reinforces the patient's dependency) may be, at least partially, an etiological factor in such dynamics. The psychological report needs to clearly present these dynamics and include not only the manner in which the subject behaves in a dependent manner, but also other manifest behavior as a result of such dynamics. An example of this for the psychological report could read:

> Mr. X is struggling with issues of autonomy versus dependency. Although he tries to separate from his mother, he is extremely dependent upon her. On a subconscious level, anxiety over insecurity exists as a result of fear of her rejection of him. His mother tends to reinforce his dependency and punishes attempts at autonomy, thus meeting her own needs relevant to her fears of being alone. Mr. X represses his anger related to his mother's control and acts these feelings out indirectly in a passive-aggressive fashion.

Position Within Family

A basic aspect of interpersonal behavior is family dynamics; or perhaps the inverse is more appropriate, that is, a basic aspect of family dynamics is interpersonal behavior. Whatever the case, it is suggested that an evaluation of family dynamics be made and included in the psychological report. As supervisors of residents and other clinical psychology trainees, we have often heard statements such as "But he doesn't have any family" or "He hasn't seen any family members in years" as a basis for questioning the inclusion of family issues in the report. Two points need to be addressed here: (a) Everyone has a "family" and (b) "family" may extend to caretakers and others who are not blood relatives and/or siblings, but who act as surrogate parents and other family members.

The first issue involves the fact that everyone, at some point, had a father and a mother. The extent to which subjects are cognizant of any relationship with the original parents could have an impact upon their psychological state. Issues of abandonment, adoption, or averse early childhood experience with parenting figures are all related to interpersonal factors which certainly can affect one's perspective of the world and manifest behaviors. Consequently, it is extremely important that psychological reports include, where possible, family dynamics, even if such dynamics do not initially appear relevant to either the evaluating psychologist or the subject of the report.

The second issue involves the fact that "significant others" can extend to older sisters, brothers, grandparents, foster parents, nannies, stepparents, and others. The criterion for being a "significant other" is more dependent upon the role played by this person than biological relationship. Consequently, when we speak of interpersonal factors within the family context, we are speaking to a broader range of possibilities of persons who play a vital role in the subject's life at present and in the past. Such information should be presented as clearly as possible in the psychological report.

Some knowledge of the family system is helpful in conceptualizing familial interpersonal dynamics. Obviously, issues of autonomy and dependence are involved as discussed previously. However, most family members tend to take on specific roles. One person may be the caretaker while another is the peacemaker. In Bowen's (1961) conceptualization of family systems, the child may take on the role as the "identified patient" as a form of scapegoating and reducing tension between the parents. Another common family dynamic is one in which one sibling is the "good" son or daughter and the other is the "bad" child. The subject may play one or more of many roles within the family complex, and there are many possibilities as to how one fits into a family context. Feelings about one's role in the family structure can have important implications relevant to social relationships. This takes on added significance if one considers issues of transference. All individuals probably distort reality to some degree, dependent upon their role within the family context and the degree to which they project. Through psychological testing and clinical observation of here-and-now behavior, clinicians can often depict the role an individual plays within the family. Such "transferential issues" are good content for this section of the psychological report.

The degree to which one feels a part of or alienated from parents, siblings, and other significant persons can also be addressed in the *interpersonal* part of the report. Not feeling part of the family structure may have strong implications for interpersonal behavior and personality development in general. Such feelings may lead to self-perceptions as one who is to be rejected or alienated. In some cases, family rejection of the subject may be appropriate, although the subject may deny his or her role in the rejection, projecting blame onto family members. Another dynamic could be that the feeling of alienation is reality and due to the pathology of a significant other. This can be seen in alcoholic families where feelings of rejection often lead to a self-concept of one who does not belong or feels flawed. Many times we have heard our patients say, "Who would want me? My own father (or mother) didn't."

Interpersonal family issues often live on as unresolved conflicts even after the death of relevant, significant others. The psychological report should address such unresolved family concerns to the extent appropriate. For example, it is not unusual for a survivor of a deceased family member to feel that he or she should have been more involved with the relative. This often is noted as an adjustment/bereavement issue. When a deeper underlying issue exists (e.g., where the subject harbors intense, unresolved resentment toward an abusive or rejecting parent), such dynamics should be described in detail and operationalized to the extent possible. The relevance of unresolved family conflicts to psychotherapy makes describing these circumstances in the psychological report a potentially useful exercise. Again, one must remember that such conflicts are not limited to "blood-related" family members, but can extend to any significant person in the subject's life.

Social Functioning and Dynamics

Overlapping with family issues are interpersonal factors related to one's position within society and self-perceptions concerning whether or not one feels a part of social situations and society in general. As is true of all interpersonal dynamics, what we see on the surface may not be the same as what an individual experiences. For example, persons may report that they have lots of friends and are "in on things." However, psychological testing may indicate that they really feel like social outcasts and are not interpersonally connected in terms of social support. Keep in mind that one's idea of a "friend" is an individualized perception. What is a friend to John may not be the same to Jim. Describing such relationships in a general social context within the psychological report is not an easy undertaking, even with the help of psychological tests.

Subjects sometimes feel alienated from the "larger" society in a very general way. They just don't seem to fit in. Schizophrenics, depressives, and many subjects with personality disorders report such feelings on clinical interview, and interpersonal detachment is often inherent in their personality dynamics. Some subjects seem not to "match-up" in a societal sense as is evident in Antisocial and Schizoid Personality Disorders. Unfortunately, these feelings of not belonging may be expressed by a rebellious or antiauthoritarian posture manifesting itself in many different ways. In the antisocial personality, the defenses are constructed in such a manner that the person "acts out" in a passive-aggressive manner. Antisocial behaviors may take on an operant flavor, reinforced by the subject gaining an identity within a peer group, although a negative one. Also, illegal acts, inappropriate aggression, or other rebellious behavior allows the subject to externalize feelings in a displacing or projecting manner. Such behaviors ultimately result in a self-defeating process for the subject. The *Interpersonal* subsection of the report is an appropriate place to discuss this type of behavior.

Dimensions of extroversion-introversion may be included as an aspect of social functioning within the psychological report. Whether or not such terms provide much clinical utility is questionable. These terms seem to be more descriptive of overt behavior and generally tell us how much the subject tends to extend out to other people or stay to himself or herself. The process of psychological functioning is not that simple. It is probably better to discuss such dynamics in terms of degree of social involvement, the extent to which the person is actually comfortable with this degree of involvement, and how the subject might react differently, depending upon the social context. Some clarity of this issue may be gained by looking at the difference between schizoid and avoidant personalities. The schizoid feels relatively comfortable (or at least not extremely anxious) about the tendency to withdraw from interpersonal and social situations. The avoidant personality, on the other hand, is uncomfortable, anxious, or unhappy about the withdrawal process. The former, for whatever reason (which may or may not be discernible), views the larger social context as not important. The avoidant views the larger social context as important and, in essence, as an attractive goal, but is unable to obtain "membership," although this is desired. The reasons behind such feelings and actions should be described in the report. It may be that some of the manifest social problems one faces (e.g., alienation, trust, or anger), may relate back to a singular or underlying interpersonal process such as loss of a loved one or abuse of a child. However, contemporary social learning processes can play a major role in maintaining behavior once it is emitted.

Social Skills

The possession of adequate social skills should also be examined. This is true both in the context of why an individual may be experiencing some difficulty interpersonally and for developing treatment. Without adequate social skills, a person tends to invite rejection: This reinforces an already existing poor self-concept. However, it is important to remember that some individuals have very good social skills and, for whatever reason, end up unhappy or developing forms of neuroses or even psychoses. One may be very adroit at verbal interaction, but unable to establish intimacy.

Social Learning Style, Manipulation, and Secondary Gains

Some subjects are manipulative either on a conscious or subconscious level. This does not necessarily have to be a sociopathic manipulation as sometimes seen in persons with Antisocial Personality Disorders, who often seem extremely sincere, but are unable to achieve appropriate or truly intimate behavior. Subconscious manipulation probably takes place in all people to one degree or another and only becomes pathological when it causes problems. An example of a well-known interpersonal manipulation is the use of guilt as a means of motivating others to meet one's own needs. Another form of manipulation is intimidation, which is frequently exhibited by paranoid subjects. Some subjects meet dependency and affectional needs through manipulative behavior. An example is the person who is hypochondriacal or who magnifies physical complaints. Such individuals call on others to be nurturing and to come to their assistance, thus meeting their dependency needs as well as alleviating their fear of abandonment. Such behavior may also be passive-aggressive, frustrating others and consequently serving as an indirect means to vent hostilities.

Manipulation may be thought of as a part of a social learning style. The premise here is that people "set-up" a repetition of an interpersonal paradigm which, although sometimes providing for interpersonal success on a short-term basis, is self-defeating in the long run. For example, the overt behavior of the subject may show a hostile nontrusting posture, coupled with cynicism and constant complaint, while psychological testing reveals that the subject has strong underlying fears of rejection and feelings of inadequacy. This subconscious self-perception is defended against by overt behavior that often results in the individual "setting himself or herself up" for rejection. Such behavior is reinforced because it validates the subject's true underlying self-image. The subject subconsciously feels rejected, stating, "See, I was right; people don't like me and don't want me around." The subject then reacts with hostility and paranoia and a vicious interpersonal cycle persists.

Another example is that of a passive-dependent housewife who doesn't drive and is married to a controlling, autocratic husband. Her seeming inadequacy dictates that her husband has to chauffeur her around, which meets her dependency needs. This reinforces a self-image as someone who can't take care of herself, leading to continued dependency and behavior which will validate this self-impression. As a result, another vicious cycle ensues. This demonstrates the interpersonal component in that both husband and wife are having needs met by their self-defeating postures. While the wife validates her dependency, the husband's self-perception as the one who is in control and takes care of things is also validated. He is figuratively and literally "in the driver's seat." This interpersonal process becomes more complex when we realize that such interplays of interpersonal behavior can take place at different levels of the personality. Certainly, the husband in the preceding example becomes frustrated on another level of personality with having to drive his wife everywhere. This serves as a means by which the wife can get back at him and is able to vent her anger in a passive-aggressive manner.

Most therapists realize that these "secondary gains" are a frequent component in human behavior. Multiple secondary gains may possibly result from one behavior. Such processes are often involved in a repetitive fashion and go together to create an interpersonal style that doesn't work for the subject and may be one of the reasons for evaluating the subject in the first place. Explaining this process in the psychological report presents a challenge, not only from the interpretative standpoint, but also from the perspective of the report writer. An example of how an interpersonal style or paradigm might be described in the psychological report follows:

> Mr. X tends to alienate himself by his hostile behavior. This causes others to either retreat from intimidation or strike back with aggression. In either case, the result is that Mr. X ends up feeling alienated and angry, believing that he has been treated unfairly. However, on an underlying level, projective testing reveals problems with trust and a fear of abandonment. Through his behavior, Mr. X is creating an interpersonal conflict which proves, on a subconscious level, that he cannot trust others and that they are rejecting or abandoning him. This has developed into a repetitive pattern which is self-defeating for Mr. X. There are secondary gains in that Mr. X can avoid undesirable, uncomfortable situations (e.g., social settings), is able to stay away from work, and can realize other pseudobenefits.

Sexual Feelings and Behaviors

Sexual feelings and behaviors, although certainly representative of intrapsychic components, are very much interpersonal. Issues of sexual identity are generally treated within the realm of self-concept and therefore are mentioned in the *Intrapsychic* subsection. How subjects relate to others on a sexual level is recommended for placement in the *Interpersonal* subsection. For example, the fact that psychological tests, in combination with clinical impressions, reveal latent sexual conflict may be treated as an intrapsychic phenomenon. However, the fact that the patient has had little or no heterosexual contact or avoids involvement on a heterosexual level more appropriately falls under the heading of "interpersonal."

Some subjects act out sexually as a means of attention seeking or manipulation. Others may use sex as a means of avoiding true intimacy, keeping things on a physical surface level. Psychopathic rapists may mix sex and aggression in an attempt to relate to the opposite sex and externalize projective distortions about relationships with significant others in their lives.

Obviously, issues of sexuality extend into areas of intimacy and trust and may require considerable integration with other interpersonal dynamics in the psychological report. How one relates sexually has great implications for overt behavior. It deserves careful consideration by the psychological report writer.

Interpersonal Conflicts

Although intrapsychic conflicts (described earlier) take place within an individual psyche, interpersonal conflicts may overtly exist between people. Conflicts with significant persons in the subject's life can take many forms. They may be seen between married couples or between casual acquaintances, in the workplace, or on the golf course. Again, it is important not to merely state that "Mr. X is experiencing marital conflict." The nature of the conflict and accompanying psychodynamics, to the extent interpretable, should be included in the report. For example, the report could read:

> Mr. X is experiencing considerable marital difficulty. He does not trust his wife and fears she will have (or has had) a relationship with another man. His hostile feelings toward her seem to alienate her further from him. On an underlying level, Mr. X is experiencing feelings of inadequacy and a fear that his wife will reject him. This appears to be, at least in part, related to his past aversive experience with significant females in his life.

We recommend the inclusion of an interpersonal segment within the *Personality Functioning* section of the psychological report and believe that what goes on between people is extremely important to psychological functioning. Issues of passive-dependency, autonomy, family dynamics, social involvement, trust, affection, and intimacy are all relevant content. Also, interpersonal conflicts and the social learning style of the subject can be described. We suggest that the length of the section be no more than one or two paragraphs, covering one-third to one-half of a page, typed and single-spaced.

CONCLUSION: PERSONALITY FUNCTIONING

The ***Personality Functioning*** section represents the "heart" of most psychological reports. This is not to belittle the importance of other sections, but to emphasize that personality assessment is a skill that is basic to psychological assessment. As indicated earlier, too often in- adequately trained report writers provide lengthy social histories and behavior observations at the expense of the ***Personality Functioning*** section. Even some neuropsychological evaluations seem to ignore the "psychological" part of the word "neuropsychological" and have very little in the report relevant to the effects of personality functioning upon intellectual and cognitive performance. No other section requires more thought, knowledge, and integrative ability than the ***Personality Functioning*** section of the report, because it is this section that fre- quently provides the most useful information to the report reader.

Chapter 5

IMPRESSIONS/DIAGNOSES

Prior to the formal *Summary and Recommendations* section of the report, a very concise statement should be made, in a separate paragraph with a separate heading, which captures the essence of the subject's diagnostic picture. Some organizations and institutions may require that this include a formal diagnostic statement per the *Diagnostic and Statistical Manual of Mental Disorders* (*DSM-IV-TR*; American Psychiatric Association, 2000). Other referral sources and organizations may not require or desire such diagnoses at all. A formal classification may not be as useful as a more descriptive impression. Tallent (1980) feels that we should not be shy about our diagnostic impressions. He also suggests that we not be "overly obsequious in suggesting a diagnosis" (p. 90). The question of whether to give a formal classification or an impression in general terms is an individual one. It is recommended that, minimally, the report provide sufficient information from which a diagnosis can easily be inferred.

This paragraph should come at the end of the *Personality Functioning* section, should be very brief, perhaps two or three sentences, and can be entitled **"Impressions."** It may include significant findings from any section of the report including the *Intellectual* and *Cognitive Functioning* section. An example of such a paragraph follows:

> Overall, Mr. X appears to be experiencing significant depression, evidenced by poor appetite, loss of interest, inactivity, and sleep disturbance. In addition, he exhibits self-destructive ideation. There is no indication of psychosis or a major thought disorder.

This provides sufficient information for other health professionals to easily infer diagnostic impressions without formally providing one and adds something beyond just giving a diagnostic label. When it is preferable to give specific diagnoses, along with corresponding codes, this can be included at the end of the ***Personality Functioning*** section by simply listing the AXIS System of the *Diagnostic and Statistical Manual of Mental Disorders* (*DSM-IV-TR*; American Psychiatric Association, 2000). An example follows:

AXIS I	-	296.22 Major Depression, Single, Episodes, Moderate
AXIS II	-	301.60 Dependent Personality Disorder
AXIS III	-	Deferred
AXIS IV	-	3 - Moderate
AXIS V	-	Current GAF: 55
		Highest GAF: 70

The clinical psychologist should defer diagnoses on AXIS III unless this information is provided by qualified medical staff.

Conclusive impressions, along with the recommendations, may be considered by some as the most important information provided by the report and should act as a "shorthand" statement depicting the relevant features of the subject's psychological state. The report writer must evaluate the setting in which he or she works, and, most importantly, the needs of the patient in providing an impression.

Chapter 6

SUMMARY AND RECOMMENDATIONS

SUMMARY

The *Summary* section of the report is important because it captures the essence of the report. It also acts as the lead into the *Recommendations* section. Some reports may have the *Summary* section at the beginning of the report with justification that this provides the reader with a quick synopsis of the important parts of the report. We believe that the *Summary* should immediately follow the results section, which seems logical and does not reinforce the idea that the reader need only read the *Summary* and not the main body of the report. Unfortunately, some readers may go directly to the *Summary* in order to save time and get to what they believe is the "important stuff." The *Summary* does not replace the main body of the report, which should contain the details that weave together psychological factors and dynamics making it relatively clear why the subject feels, thinks, and acts as he or she does.

We suggest that the *Summary* section of the report be contained within one paragraph which covers about one-third, but no more than one-half, of a page and presented in a separate section labeled "**Summary.**" The *Summary* section is where the report writer reiterates the major findings of the report. Nothing should be included in the *Summary* section that has not been addressed in the main body of the report. Obviously the inverse is not true. The *Summary* can repeat some of the statements that are in the main body of the report or it can use language that is similar and means the same as that which is in the main part of the report. We prefer to repeat the salient findings relatively verbatim to assure that we are capturing what the main body of the report states. Relevant background information may also be included if it relates to the psychological findings, although background information should not dominate this section. For example, the *Personality Functioning* section of the report may state that the subject experiences significant depression and self-destructive tendencies, while the *Background Information* section might reveal that the subject has attempted suicide. It would be appropriate to mention in the *Summary* that he or she has attempted suicide, in the past, along with the findings from the *Personality Functioning* section.

More specifically, the *Summary* section should start with a statement of the basic demographics of the subject coupled with the reason for the referral for evaluation. This can be accomplished in one sentence. Next the *Summary* could include a statement about general orientation, level of intellect, and cognitive functioning. Personality factors can follow including the ruling in or out of psychosis or a major mental illness. Bizarre symptoms such as hallucinations or delusions should be reported along with other indications of personality disorganization (e.g., looseness of association or tangential thought). Emotional states such as depression and anxiety should also be discussed here with some interpretive analysis about major conflicts or primary defenses used (e.g., repressed anger, projection, etc.). Interpersonal dynamics should also be included such as social posture, alienation, and trust issues. Important familial relationships can also be included. High-risk areas should be addressed (e.g., suicidal and homicidal ideation, explosiveness, and/or tendency to decompensate under stress). This section should include anything that is in the main results sections which the author feels deserves emphasizing to the reader.

RECOMMENDATIONS

The *Recommendations* section of the report takes information from the results sections and translates this into a suggested plan of action. This section answers the question "Now that we know this about the subject, what can be done to help?" This section should lay out in practical terms how the salient findings of the results might be addressed. Too often, the reader will take the journey through the report to find an anticlimactic *Recommendations* section that is vague and offers little in the way of concrete suggestions for intervention. For example, some reports may state only that the subject should receive some form of intervention (e.g., "referral to individual therapy" or "Subject needs to improve interpersonal skills"). We believe that the psychologist has a great deal to offer in terms of specifics of interventions which could prove beneficial to the subject and those professionals attempting to help him or her. We suggest that this section be highly focused and behaviorally specific. Problem areas, strengths, or other considerations for recommendations may be derived not only from formal test results but also from information provided by a mental status exam and collateral sources. For example, testing may show that the subject experiences considerable underlying hostility, while reports from family members may indicate the subject has frequent emotional outbursts. At the same time, the mental status exam may reveal that the subject denies ever having hostile feelings. The *Recommendations* section should use all three sources of information to provide support that the problem is worthy of intervention with suggestions for addressing the problem.

The Management of
Specific Areas of Concern

The *Recommendations* section should cover a page or more and list, by number, the salient issues discovered in the report to be the focus of intervention. The list of areas to be addressed should begin with the most important. Each issue discussed should include a brief statement of the issue and why it represents a concern. This should be followed by recommendations for managing the area of concern. If the results indicate that Mr. Patient is experiencing personality disorganization with psychotic symptoms, has problems with aggression, and has been abusing drugs, these are relatively serious findings that demand almost immediate attention and intense intervention. For these concerns, the *Recommendations* section might begin with a lead-off sentence such as "Specific areas of concern are discussed below with recommendations for each" and then list each area to be addressed, why each area is of concern, and recommendations for each concern listed. For example:

1. ***Significant Personality Disorganization:*** Psychological assessment indicates that Mr. Patient is currently experiencing significant personality disorganization. He appears to have lost contact with reality and is delusional. He has command hallucinations which have told him to emit destructive behaviors. This represents significant risk for Mr. Patient and those persons involved with him. He could act on his distorted thinking in such a manner as to represent a danger to himself or others. Hospitalization is recommended with the goal of stabilization of his psychiatric symptoms and protection from harm. It is also recommended that Mr. Patient be evaluated for medication as a component of stabilization. After stabilization is achieved, individual and group therapies are recommended to address areas of concern as described below.

2. ***Aggression:*** This assessment revealed that Mr. Patient experiences considerable underlying hostility which he is likely to discharge externally. Collateral reports reveal that he has been in several physical altercations and that he has poor impulse control. As indicated above, his thinking is currently disorganized, which increases the likelihood that he could employ poor judgment, to include psychotic thinking, and represent a danger to himself and others. After stabilization is achieved and while in a secure environment, it is recommended that he participate in intervention for anger management. Also, individual therapy could address with Mr. Patient his hostility and attempt to assist him in venting his anger within the context of a therapeutic environment. In addition, evaluation for medication that addresses his hostility and emotional lability is recommended.

3. ***Substance Abuse:*** Mr. Patient has had significant difficulty with substance abuse. He has been ar-

rested for possession of marijuana and has admitted to almost daily use of this drug. This psychological evaluation indicates that Mr. Patient is
likely to employ escape behavior as a defense
against unwanted feelings. Given this defensive
structure, he is likely to use drugs/alcohol as a
means of escaping unwanted feelings (i.e., he self-
medicates). Alcohol/drug use represents a significant problem for Mr. Patient for several reasons.
The use of substances tends to weaken ego controls and can contribute to personality decompensation, resulting in psychosis. Drugs and/or alcohol can interact with prescribed medication and
diminish, or negatively alter, the potentially positive effects of medication. Substance involvement
disinhibits emotional controls, which can result
in poor judgment and impulsive behavior. Alco-
hol/drug involvement can also contribute to association with negative peer influences and illegal
behavior as well as assist the subject in denial and
avoiding addressing important issues. It can also
retard psychological growth. It is recommended
that Mr. Patient receive a specialized substance
abuse assessment with intervention as indicated.
Given the gravity of substance involvement for
Mr. Patient and his lack of compliance with drug
treatment in the past, random drug screens are also
recommended.

A myriad of possible areas of concern could be gleaned from a
psychological evaluation. We have found that it is generally typical to
find between five and seven different areas of concern to be addressed.
In some ways these "areas of concern" represent some elements of risk
in that, if they are not addressed, risk for the subject to repeat inappropriate behavior and continue to have problems remains high and could
escalate. The important thing is that we identify these areas and develop effective management strategies for the reduction of risk. Specific content areas for recommendations are many and it would be nearly

impossible to list them all. Below we have attempted to list some of the more common areas of concern.

- Personality Disorganization/Psychosis
- Depression/Anxiety
- Neuropsychological Impairment
- Learning Disability
- Substance Abuse/Dependance
- Aggression/Anger
- School Issues
- Poor Interpersonal Skills
- Denial, Minimization, and Lack of Insight
- Poor Judgment, Impulsivity, and Low Frustration Tolerances
- Family/Marital/Other Interpersonal Conflicts
- Trust and Paranoia
- Self-/Other-Destructive Ideation
- Isolation
- Self-Concept Problems
- Medical Issues
- Medical Issues Contributing to Psychological Problems (and Vice Versa)
- Authority Problems/Psychopathy
- Sexual Issues
- Compliance With Treatment/Medication

Immediate Needs

Certain findings almost always require immediate attention. Suicidal/homicidal ideation or significant medical issues might require that the psychologist postpone the formal writing of the report in order to take action. The same is true for subjects who are found to be unable to care for themselves for clinical reasons. These concerns, although not usually the focus of the report, could be part of any psychological assessment, and the psychologist must be prepared to take action for the protection of the subject and others. Procedures for addressing such high-risk areas should be developed beforehand with names and numbers of mental health professionals who can admit to a hospital as well as the means by which one can elicit help from police and crisis intervention services. This is part of what we do as psychologists, and we must be psychologically and logistically ready to accept this responsibility. When immediate action is taken, an explanation of this should be included in the *Recommendations* section.

The Integration of Strengths

The preceding seems to emphasize the pathological aspects of the findings. To some degree, this is appropriate; we are trying to find out what the problems are so we can possibly do something about them. However, it is also appropriate to develop recommendations from factors that can decrease or eliminate the magnitude of problems and increase the opportunity for positive outcome. For example, if the report indicates that an adolescent subject is of high intelligence, this can be important information to use in an academic setting to establish positive expectations and, possibly, augment the subject's self-concept. A recommendation integrating subject strengths might read as follows:

> 4. *School Issues:* Assessment indicates that Mr. Patient experiences significant difficulty in high school. His grades are failing and he has had attendance problems. On the test of intelligence, Mr. Patient scored within the High Average Range, and on a screening test of academic achievement, he scored above a high school level for both reading and spelling. Given these scores, Mr. Patient appears to have the intellectual potential and academic achievement to perform well in school. This information can be provided to Mr. Patient as a means of creating a positive expectation and, possibly, increasing his self-image. With his abilities in mind, goals for school performance and subsequent education/training can be established.

There are many other positive attributes that can be woven into recommendations which could be helpful to the subject and those persons involved with him or her. Good social skills, a positive work history, and special talents (e.g., music, sports, or empathy for others) are just a few of the many positive attributes that a psychological evaluation could discover and integrate into recommendations.

Other Hints for Recommendations

Sometimes results do not require immediate action of a crisis nature. However, it may be appropriate (or just courteous) to make a phone call or personal visit to a referent to provide a preview of the preliminary findings of the evaluation before the final report is written. This may be necessary in specific cases such as when results need to be made known as soon as possible or deadlines have to be met. For example, findings may reveal indications of organic involvement with a need for neurological evaluation. By waiting for a formal report, procedures that could prove helpful to the subject would be delayed. Findings may reveal key content for therapy, and the therapist could initiate interventions with the information provided by the psychological evaluation without having to wait to have the formal report. By contacting the referent with some "immediate feedback," the report writer has an opportunity to evaluate if the findings to be reported are the most appropriate and if other information might be included in the report. A referent may suggest ideas the report writer had not thought of which could be deserving of further exploration. Customer satisfaction is important. Obviously, when information is shared, guidelines for confidentiality must be observed.

Recommendations should be stated in behavioral terms to the extent possible. Step-by-step descriptions can help convey exactly the meaning of the recommendation. Vague and generalized statements should be avoided. The general rule is "The more specific the better." For example, to just state "It is recommended that Mr. Patient receive treatment for depression" does not provide much direction for the professional who is to work with the subject in treatment. Of greater utility is the statement:

> It is recommended that Mr. Patient receive individual psychotherapy to address his depression. He appears to have withdrawn and lost interest in activities he once enjoyed. Behavioral programming to develop a repertoire of active involvement for Mr. Patient may prove beneficial. He also appears to be grieving the loss of his mother. These issues could be addressed in therapy. Given the long-term nature of his depression, evaluation for medication is recommended.

Making definitive predictions is discouraged. No one can predict how another human will react under certain circumstances. To report that someone is "mildly, moderately, or severely" suicidal may certainly alert others to the problem; however, one person's perception of "mild" may be very different from another's. Placing persons in high- to low-risk categories is tricky business and has inherent problems. This does not mean that we do not attempt to indicate when persons represent a significant threat, but more is needed to clarify some of the rationale behind our thinking. We have found it helpful to subjects and readers to list those areas of concern that represent risk, explain why this represents a risk for the subject, and then recommend means for managing the risk.

Chapter 7

CONCLUSION

Before the final psychological report is sent to the referent, we suggest a critical reading by a colleague or supervisor. When the report writer is a student (e.g., intern or postdoctoral trainee), this process should be automatically built into the supervisory process. However, when no formal supervisory relationship exists, there is a tendency to not take the time or avoid the additional scrutiny of another pair of eyes. Issues of countertransference and bias hold true for psychological reports as they do for therapy. The objectivity provided by a third party can be extremely beneficial to the final report. A third party may provide a different perspective for consideration by the report writer. This individual can also act as a proofreader for grammatical, spelling, and other errors. Too many misspelled words and poor grammar can make a good evaluation appear bad. The report should be "clean."

The format that we have presented in this text emphasizes a practical and structured approach to writing the psychological report. We want to emphasize that one size rarely fits all, and variations in reports will be necessary depending on setting and clinical need. However, we believe that many of the principles and procedures outlined in this book can be generalized to most settings and subjects. Finally, we want to emphasize that continual practice and supervision probably represent the most effective training for the writing of a quality psychological report.

APPENDICES

Appendix A

PSYCHOLOGICAL EVALUATION FORMAT: GUIDELINE QUESTIONS

The following questions are to aid in completing psychological evaluations and represent the type of information to be included in each section. Obviously, not all questions would be appropriate for all patients, nor should these lists be considered exhaustive. Specifics for each section are discussed in the text.

A. **REASON FOR REFERRAL:**

Who referred the subject and for what reasons? Be as specific as possible about the referral question.

B. **NOTIFICATION OF PURPOSE AND LIMITS OF CONFIDENTIALITY:**

What is the purpose of the evaluation and who will be potential users of the report? A statement should be included that this has been explained to the subject and the subject's level of understanding of the purpose and limits of confidentiality of the evaluation.

C. **EVALUATION INSTRUMENTS AND SOURCES OF INFORMATION:**

What tests were administered? Also, include any other sources of information (i.e., review of reports, interviews with family members, subject interview, etc.).

D. BACKGROUND INFORMATION:

(The *Background Information* section of the report should be relatively brief with the majority of the report reflecting psychological functioning.)

Subject Demographics and Developmental History

1. What is the age, sex, marital status, and race of the subject?
2. Was subject's birth normal?
3. Did the subject meet developmental milestones at age-appropriate times?
4. Any history of early childhood trauma (e.g., sexual/physical abuse)?
5. Other significant childhood/developmental issues?

Familial History and Significant Relationships

1. Where and with whom is the subject living?
2. What is the subject's marital situation?
3. Does the subject have living parents?
4. Does the subject have children/siblings?
5. What is the nature of significant familial relationships?
6. Is the subject involved in other significant relationships?
7. Does the subject experience any sexual difficulties?

Education and Employment History

1. What is the subject's occupation and educational level?
2. How has the subject functioned in these areas?
3. How did the subject function in school, academically and behaviorally? Truancy?
4. Did the subject participate in Special Education Programming or is he or she learning disabled?
5. What has been the subject's employment history?
6. Was the subject in the military?
7. Does the subject receive any benefits (e.g., Social Security income)?

Medical and Psychiatric History

1. Does the subject have any significant physical problems, especially those which could contribute to emotional/behavioral problems (e.g., head injury, thyroid problems, history of seizures, etc.)? (Be sure to cite sources of any medical information.)

2. Has the subject had a history of psychiatric problems?
3. Has the subject ever been hospitalized psychiatrically?
4. Has the subject ever been involved in outpatient therapy?
5. Does the subject take any psychotropic medications?
6. Has subject ever been diagnosed with a psychiatric disorder? What disorder?
7. Explain circumstances for affirmative answers on one to five above.
8. What symptoms has the subject exhibited recently and in the past?

Alcohol and Drug History

1. What has been the subject's history with drugs/alcohol, including type, frequency, amount, and impact on subject's life?

Other Relevant History

1. Is there any other background information that could be pertinent to the evaluation (e.g., legal issues, sexual behavior, interpersonal issues, or avocational pursuits)?

Factors Prompting Referral

1. What were the concerns/behaviors that prompted the evaluation? This should include some of the same information reported in the *Reason for Referral* section of the report but should provide more detail if available.

E.   BEHAVIORAL OBSERVATIONS:

(This section should be relatively brief and attempt to describe the subject's behavior as observed. The *Behavioral Observations* section of the report is not the place for drawing inferences from the behavior emitted.)

1. Did the subject arrive on time? Accompanied by whom?
2. How was the subject dressed (neat, loud-color clothes, shirt unbuttoned to the navel, etc.)?
3. How was the subject's personal hygiene (well kept, clean)?
4. What was the subject's physical appearance?
5. Did the subject appear motivated to participate in the assessment process?
6. Did the subject complete all test tasks asked of him or her? If not, what was omitted, resisted, and/or refused?
7. Did the subject exhibit any problems with vision or hearing?

8. How did the subject approach the testing situation (guardedly, openly, enjoying the process, struggling, seemed stressed)?
9. Were there any difficulties in establishing rapport?
10. Did the subject exhibit any unusual motor behavior?
11. Did the subject react differently to different stimuli (e.g., when presented Rorschach Cards, did the subject block)?
12. Did the subject exhibit bizarre behaviors such as hallucinations or delusions?
13. Did the subject exhibit problems with ambulation, apraxia, or other motor skills?
14. Did the subject seem to comprehend what was said to him or her?
15. Did the subject speak openly or guardedly during the clinical interview?
16. Did the subject react differently to emotionally laden content areas (e.g., change of affect when talking about lost love objects)?
17. Other observations?

F. INTELLECTUAL AND COGNITIVE FUNCTIONING:

1. Was the subject oriented as to time, person, place, and situation?
2. Did the subject exhibit sensory-perceptual problems?
3. Was the subject able to focus and maintain attention and/or concentration? If not, is this due to psychological interference or possible neurological involvement?
4. What was the subject's general level of intellectual functioning?
5. Was there a significant verbal/performance subtest difference? Is there significant intra-/intersubtest scatter?
6. How did the subject score on subtests measuring general fund of information and vocabulary?
7. How did the subject's level of academic achievement compare to his or her level of intellect?
8. How was the subject's visual organizational functioning? Visuomotor organization functioning?
9. Any impairment in visuomotor speed?
10. What was the subject's abstracting ability? Was he or she concrete?
11. Was the subject able to perform calculations adequately?
12. What was the subject's memory functioning, in terms of immediate, recent, and remote memories?
13. What was the subject's language functioning, in terms of general expressive and receptive language?
14. Were there any indications of anomia, agnosia, or other word-finding problems?
15. Were there any indications of other neuropsychological signs (i.e., perseveration, confabulation, catastrophic reaction)?

16. Were there any physical indications of neurological involvement (blurred vision, headaches, numbness, etc.)?
17. Were emotional factors interfering with subject's cognitive efficiency?
18. Overall, were there indications of possible neuropsychological involvement?
19. In summary, what are the salient findings for this section (i.e., level of intelligence, cognitive impairments and strengths, academic achievement [literacy])?

G. PERSONALITY FUNCTIONING:*

1. **Emotional Factors** (past and present overt behavior and mental status):

   a. Was the subject oriented to person, place, time, and situation? (May have been placed in the **Intellectual and Cognitive Functioning** section.)
   b. What was the affective state of the subject (appropriate, inappropriate, flat, labile, blocking, hypomanic, etc.)?
   c. Did the subject report any significant emotional stress (from interview, observation, and/or objective personality test, e.g., MMPI-2)?
   d. What was the prevailing mood of the subject (sadness, hostility, paranoia)? Was there a combination of any of these on the surface?
   e. Did the subject exhibit illogical sentence sequence, looseness of association, flight of ideas, or pressured speech?
   f. Did the subject exhibit delusions, hallucinations, feelings of depersonalization, or other signs of loss of reality contact?
   g. Did projective testing or other indicators reveal that the subject has decompensated in the past or has become extremely depressed and/or manic?
   h. Were there other overt behavioral indications (i.e., histrionics, withdrawal, fearful, etc.)?
   i. What was the subject's ability to modulate affect (Rorschach)?
   j. Did the subject report feelings of depression, loss of appetite, sleep disturbance, loss of interest, mania, or other indications of affective disturbance?

---

*NOTE: The *Emotional, Intrapsychic*, and *Interpersonal* subsections of the *Personality Functioning* section do not require headings. The same is true for the *Summary* and *Recommendations* subsections under the *Summary and Recommendations* section.

      k.   Did the subject report suicidal/homicidal ideation in the past or present? To what extent? What was the nature of these ideations?

      l.   What other overt behavior/emotions did the subject exhibit?

2. Intrapsychic:

      a.   Did test data reveal denied or repressed affect?

      b.   Did assessment indicate underlying hostility or depression?

      c.   Does the subject tend to internalize/externalize feelings?

      d.   Does the subject act out his or her feelings in a passive-aggressive manner?

      e.   Did testing reveal underlying tensions?

      f.   What are the subject's major conflicts and sources of anxieties (sexual, marital, autonomy, trust)?

      g.   What are the major defenses utilized by the client? What purpose do these defenses serve? How do they manifest themselves?

      h.   Does the subject exhibit delusions, hallucinations, or illusions? What symbolic purpose do they serve in terms of the intrapsychic structure (i.e., hearing a voice to harm oneself)?

      i.   What is the subject's self-image? Are there underlying feelings of inadequacy or inferiority?

      j.   Did test data reveal latent self-destructive signs?

      k.   Does the subject have any insight into his or her difficulties?

      l.   To what extent is the subject willing to accept responsibility for his or her behavior?

      m.   What other psychological forces are working intrapsychically (i.e., obsessions, compulsions, guilt, etc.)?

3. Interpersonal:

      a.   Does the subject appear to be interpersonally passive and/or dependent? Is the subject an independent person?

      b.   Are there autonomy versus dependency issues?

      c.   What is the subject's psychological position within the family structure? Systems issues? Does he or she feel alienated from family?

      d.   Are there particular family members for which the subject has unresolved feelings?

      e.   Does the subject feel he or she fits into society as part of a social group or does he or she feel alienated, rebellious, and/or antiauthoritarian?

      f.   Is the subject schizoid/avoidant or is he or she extroverted and socially comfortable?

g. Are there issues of unmet affection and dependency needs?

h. What is the subject's social-learning approach (i.e., what kind of behaviors does the subject emit that set him or her up for rejection and subsequent alienation)? Are there secondary gains?

i. What is the level of the subject's social skills?

j. Are trust issues evident? In terms of social learning, how did such trust issues begin? Are there abandonment issues or rejection concerns?

k. Is there marital conflict and/or conflict with significant others? How do such conflicts manifest themselves?

l. What other interpersonal issues seem relevant?

H. IMPRESSIONS:

What diagnosis(es) is (are) appropriate for this subject? Briefly, what are the major findings concerning this subject's psychological state? (Report in a few sentences.)

I. SUMMARY AND RECOMMENDATIONS:

1. Summary

a. What major points under each of the previous sections are most salient and best describe the subject's psychological state?

2. Recommendations

a. What are the primary areas of concerns as indicated by the results of the evaluation? List each area of concern separately and include for each area:

(1) What is the current status of each of these areas of concern as indicated from testing, clinical interview, and other sources of information?

(2) What are viable means of addressing each area of concern (e.g., medication, therapies, referral for specialized services)? Be specific about different intervention strategies. What is the prognosis for each intervention?

(3) What are the immediate needs of the subject and recommendations for addressing these (e.g., suicidal precautions, medical intervention, hospitalization, etc.)?

b. What strengths might contribute to a positive outcome, and how could they be integrated into treatment (e.g., reliable work history, good social skills, intelligence, etc.)?

    c.   What would be the most appropriate way for hospital staff, teachers, and others to respond to this subject (e.g., differential reinforcement of nondelusional thinking, passive but friendly, kind firmness, etc.)?

    d.   What is the subject's prognosis? What are the indicators for this prognosis?

    e.   Are there any other recommendations appropriate for this subject?

Appendix B

PSYCHOLOGICAL EVALUATION FORMAT*

The following is a suggested format for the psychological report. Space has been allowed for writing notes under each heading of the outline. Data may not be available for each area outlined. However, the evaluator should attempt to cover as many of the areas as possible addressing additional areas as indicated. The final report can be written/dictated from this outline.

CONFIDENTIAL PSYCHOLOGICAL EVALUATION

NAME: _____

DATE OF BIRTH: _____ MARITAL STATUS: _____

AGE: _____ OCCUPATION or STUDENT STATUS: _____

SEX: _____ DATE(S) OF EVALUATION: _____

REASON FOR REFERRAL (From where and/or whom the subject was referred and why):

_____
_____
_____
_____
_____
_____
_____
_____
_____

*This form may be reproduced for professional use; however, any commercial use or widespread distribution is prohibited.

NOTIFICATION OF PURPOSE AND LIMITS OF CONFIDENTIALITY:

_____

_____

_____

_____

_____

EVALUATION INSTRUMENTS AND SOURCES OF INFORMATION

(Include all evaluative procedures, including tests, interviews, review of reports, etc.):

_____

_____

_____

_____

_____

_____

BACKGROUND INFORMATION:

Subject Demographics and Developmental History:

_____

_____

_____

_____

_____

_____

_____

Familial History and Significant Relationships:

_____

_____

_____

_____

_____

_____

_____

Education and Employment History:

_____

_____

_____

_____

_____

_____

_____

Medical and Psychiatric History:

_____

_____

_____

_____

_____

_____

_____

Alcohol and Drug History:

_____

_____

_____

_____

_____

_____

_____

Other Relevant History:

_____

_____

_____

_____

_____

_____

_____

Factors Prompting Referral:

_____

_____

_____

_____

_____

_____

_____

BEHAVIORAL OBSERVATIONS (Examples: timeliness, appearance, co-operativeness, eye contact, problems seeing or hearing, frustration level, if completes tasks, approach to testing, motivation, motor behavior, problems with rapport, passive participation, overly active, bizarre behavior):

_____

_____

_____

_____

_____

_____

_____

_____

_____

_____

_____

_____

_____

_____

INTELLECTUAL AND COGNITIVE FUNCTIONING (Examples: orientation, sensory-perceptual, IQ, verbal-performance differences, inter-/intrasubtest scatter, fund of general information, vocabulary, academic achievement level and its relationship to level of intelligence, focus, attention, concentration, abstractions/concreteness, calculating, judgment, visual organization, visuomotor organization, visuomotor speed, confabulation, other signs of possible neurological/cognitive impairment):

PERSONALITY FUNCTIONING:*

Emotional Factors (Examples: past and present overt behavior, orientation, affective level, hallucinations, delusions, looseness of associations, tangential, incoherent, illogical, pressured speech, agitated, anxious depression, suicidal/homicidal ideations past and present, potential for decompensation under stress):

_____

_____

_____

_____

_____

_____

_____

_____

_____

_____

_____

_____

_____

Intrapsychic (Examples: denied or repressed affect, ego structure, i.e., major defenses and how used, tensions and conflicts, hallucinations or delusions, insight, self-image):

_____

_____

_____

_____

_____

_____

_____

_____

_____

_____

_____

_____

_____

*NOTE: The *Emotional, Intrapsychic,* and *Interpersonal* subsections of the *Personality Functioning* section do not require headings. The same is true for the *Summary* and *Recommendations* subsections under the *Summary and Recommendations* section.

Interpersonal (Examples: relationship issues, dependent/independent, family/marital dynamics, trust issues, social dynamics, sexual involvement, social skills/social comfortableness:

_____
_____
_____
_____
_____
_____
_____
_____
_____
_____
_____
_____
_____

IMPRESSIONS (Diagnostic impression, reality contact, self-/other-destructive potentials):

_____
_____
_____
_____

SUMMARY AND RECOMMENDATIONS (Salient psychological features from above):

_____
_____
_____
_____
_____
_____
_____
_____
_____
_____
_____
_____
_____
_____
_____

Recommendations (List each concern to be addressed separately and numbered with the concern that appears to be the most important issue listed first, second most important listed second, and so on. Include with each area of concern the current status of these concerns and specific strategies addressing each area. Include prognosis if appropriate. Address immediate needs, e.g., suicidal, medical, and follow up. Include strengths and how these could be integrated into recommendations to enhance probability of positive outcome, e.g., reliable work history):

_____

_____

_____

_____

_____

_____

_____

_____

_____

_____

_____

_____

_____

_____

_____

_____

_____

_____

_____

_____

_____

_____

_____

_____

_____

_____

_____

_____

_____

Appendix C

EXAMPLE:

CONFIDENTIAL
PSYCHOLOGICAL EVALUATION*

NAME: Jane Q. Patient   **OCCUPATION:** Unemployed

DATE OF BIRTH: 8/26/73   **MARITAL STATUS:** Single

AGE: 28   **REFERRAL SOURCE:** H. E. Goode, PhD,
                                         Clinical Psychologist

SEX: Female
                                      DATE OF EVALUATION: 9/21/01

REASON FOR REFERRAL: Ms. Jane Q. Patient was referred for psychological evaluation by H. E. Goode, PhD, Clinical Psychologist and the subject's
therapist. Dr. Goode stated that Ms. Patient has been experiencing problems
with sleep and appetite and has been complaining of problems with concentration. He stated that she has been having crying spells and reports feeling
sad much of the time. Dr. Goode also reported that Ms. Patient has reported
hearing "voices." Dr. Goode requested evaluation to differentiate between
psychosis and major depression as well as to assist with clarification of psychodynamic factors.

**NOTIFICATION OF PURPOSE AND LIMITS OF CONFIDENTIAL-
ITY:** The purpose of the report was explained to Ms. Patient as well as the
limits of confidentiality. She was told that the report would be sent to Dr.
Goode, her therapist, and possibly used to assist with her treatment. She indicated that she understood and agreed to continue with the assessment.

---

*Because of the size of the pages in this book, this sample report is longer than the recom-
mended four to six pages suggested by the authors.

PAGE #
CONFIDENTIAL PSYCHOLOGICAL EVALUATION
JANE Q. PATIENT
SEPTEMBER 21, 2001

EVALUATION INSTRUMENTS AND SOURCES OF INFORMATION:
Wechsler Adult Intelligence Scale-Third Edition (WAIS-III); Wide Range
Achievement Test, Third Revision (WRAT-3); Bender-Gestalt; Minnesota
Multiphasic Personality Inventory, Second Edition (MMPI-2); Rorschach Ink-
blot Technique; Thematic Apperception Test (TAT); Incomplete Sentences;
Kinetic Family Drawing; interviews with subject, Jane Q. Patient, and subject's
mother and father, Mary and George Patient; consultation with H. E. Goode,
Clinical Psychologist (subject's therapist), review of subject's medical records
from Central County Hospital; review Social History (MSW, 4/24/00).

BACKGROUND INFORMATION:

Subject Demographics and Developmental History: Jane Q. Patient is a
28-year-old, single, Caucasian female who lives in Anytown, USA with her
parents, Mary and George Patient. According to Mrs. Patient (mother), the
subject's birth was uncomplicated and she met developmental milestones at
age-appropriate times. Mrs. Patient also reported that her daughter "was a
rather shy child" who had few friends and would "prefer to be alone." She
went on to report that Ms. Patient dated one male peer in high school and this
relationship lasted for about 6 months. Mrs. Patient stated that she does not
believe that her daughter has ever been the victim of physical or sexual abuse.
Ms. Patient reported the same. The subject's mother also stated that Ms. Patient has an older brother, age 37, who is currently married and, reportedly,
doing well. Mrs. Patient is a housewife and her husband is retired from the
military.

Familial History and Significant Relationships: Ms. Patient has not been
married nor does she have children. She reported that since high school, she
has been in two relationships, both of short duration. She described these
relationships as "unsatisfactory" and that the males with whom she was involved had "many problems." She described her relationship with her parents
as "OK" but "distant." She reported that she currently has one "friend" with
whom she "has dinner or goes to a movie once in a while."

Education and Employment History: Ms. Patient reported that she is a high
school graduate. She also stated she did not participate in special education
classes nor was she diagnosed as learning disabled. She reported that her grades
were "good - mostly A's and B's." Her mother indicated that Ms. Patient was

PAGE #
CONFIDENTIAL PSYCHOLOGICAL EVALUATION
JANE Q. PATIENT
SEPTEMBER 21, 2001

not a behavioral problem in school but "stayed mostly to herself." She further stated the subject played an instrument in the band for 1 year but stopped in order "to concentrate on her grades." Ms. Patient enrolled in college but left school after 2 years citing "emotional problems" as her reason for not continuing. She is currently unemployed but has held a variety of jobs including secretary, sales clerk, and legal assistant. Her longest period of employment was 6 months; however, her mother indicated that when she did work, she was a reliable and conscientious employee. She does not receive any form of benefits nor was she in the military.

Medical and Psychiatric History: Ms. Patient reported, and her mother confirmed, that she has no known major medical problems. Both the subject and her mother denied that Ms. Patient has ever experienced seizures, significant head trauma, diabetes, hypertension, or thyroid problems. Her mother reported that she had "asthma as a child" but "outgrew it." Ms. Patient did report that "Sometimes, I have bad headaches and feel light-headed." Ms. Patient has a documented history of psychiatric problems for approximately the last 10 years. Her medical records indicate that she first experienced emotional problems in 1991 concurrent with self-destructive ideation. At that time, she was hospitalized at Central County Hospital for 30 days and was given a discharge diagnosis of Major Depression, Single Episode. She was placed on Zoloft, an antidepressant, with follow-up care with the Anywhere Community Mental Health Center. Her compliance with medication and attendance for therapy was described as "poor." Ms. Patient was again hospitalized on 7/3/97 for a period of 2 weeks. She had cut her wrist in an apparent suicide attempt. This attempt was described as "serious," requiring several sutures. Ms. Patient has been in outpatient therapy with H. E. Goode, PhD, for the past 3 months and is currently hospitalized following another suicide attempt (i.e., again cutting her wrist).

Alcohol and Drug History: Ms. Patient, according to her medical records and her mother, has used alcohol excessively during "binge drinking." Ms. Patient admitted to use but indicated that she only "has a few beers on the weekend at the most." She also reported that she has tried marijuana in the past. She denied any other drug/alcohol involvement.

Factors Prompting Referral: As indicated above, Ms. Patient is currently hospitalized following a suicide attempt. Her therapist, Dr. Goode, reported

PAGE #
CONFIDENTIAL PSYCHOLOGICAL EVALUATION
JANE Q. PATIENT
SEPTEMBER 21, 2001

that she had been missing her therapy appointments and not taking her medi-cation. He also reported that when he did see her, she appeared to be experi-encing problems with concentration, sleep, and appetite and reported that she felt sad much of the time. He further stated that she had again been hearing voices of a self-deprecating nature (e.g., "You don't deserve to live"). Dr. Goode referred Ms. Patient for psychological evaluation to aid in clarification of diagnosis and to assist in determining psychological dynamics.

BEHAVIORAL OBSERVATIONS: Ms. Patient arrived to the evaluation session on time. She was brought by a mental health technician on the staff of the hospital in which the evaluation took place. She was neatly dressed and hygiene good. She stands approximately 5 ft. 6 in. tall and she reported that she weighs about 150 lbs. The purpose of the evaluation was explained to Ms. Patient. She was told a report would be developed concerning her psycho-logical functioning and the results shared with her therapist, Dr. Goode, and possibly other staff of the hospital involved in her treatment. She indicated that she understood and agreed to continue with the assessment. Ms. Patient completed all test tasks asked of her and she was cooperative throughout the assessment. She gave poor eye contact, spoke in a soft, hesitant voice, and offered little verbally beyond that which was asked of her. She seemed to easily comprehend instructions but did not initiate tasks or conversation on her own. Periodically, Ms. Patient had to be refocused on the task and tended to stare off into space. When she did offer spontaneous comment, she spoke in a self-deprecating manner about herself and her life. During the clinical interview, Ms. Patient answered questions but seemed reluctant to offer infor-mation about her feelings and thoughts. Ms. Patient did not exhibit grossly inappropriate behavior, such as delusions or hallucinations, during the entire evaluation.

INTELLECTUAL AND COGNITIVE FUNCTIONING: Ms. Patient was oriented to time, person, and place. She also was aware of the circumstances under which she was evaluated. Ms. Patient's sensory-perceptual functioning seemed intact, although she reported that she sometimes wears glasses; how-ever, she also reported that she did not need them most of the time and did not appear to have any difficulty seeing items related to the testing. Her concen-tration and attention appeared impaired, probably as the result of emotional problems.

PAGE #
CONFIDENTIAL PSYCHOLOGICAL EVALUATION
JANE Q. PATIENT
SEPTEMBER 21, 2001

On the test of intelligence, Ms. Patient scored a Verbal IQ of 118, a Performance IQ of 102, and a Full Scale IQ of 109. This places her at the upper end of the Average Range of intelligence. Subtest Scale Scores are as follows:

VERBAL		PERFORMANCE	
Information	14	Picture Completion	12
Similarities	12	Picture Arrangement	11
Vocabulary	15	Block Design	9
Arithmetic	11	Digit Symbol	11
Comprehension	12	Matrix Reasoning	9
Digit Span	14		

A disparity of 16 points between Verbal and Performance Subtests was evident, likely due, at least in part, to psychomotor retardation related to motor slowness and possibly the effects of medication. Given this, it is estimated that Ms. Patient's potential level of intellect likely falls within the High Average Range. Ms. Patient scored highest on subtests of the test of intelligence which have been found to measure one's vocabulary and fund of general information as well as the ability to recall material immediately after it has been presented. She scored significantly above average on these subtests. She scored somewhat above average on subtests measuring the performance of verbal abstractions, the ability to evaluate a situation and respond appropriately, and the capacity to discern the important details from a total situation. Her next highest scores, which were slightly above average, were on subtests that measure the ability to perform mental math, employ eye-hand motor coordination and speed, and arrange events in an appropriate sequence. She scored just below average on subtests of the test of intelligence that assess visual organization and visuomotor organization.

Ms. Patient's immediate, recent, and remote memories appeared intact, although she reported that she has difficulty remembering recent events. This seems likely to be related to some difficulty with concentration as the result of emotional factors. Ms. Patient, at times, exhibited some difficulties with attention but was quite capable of remaining focused on task. Her capacity to express herself and understand what was said also seemed intact. On a screening test of academic achievement, she scored on a college level for both read-

PAGE #
CONFIDENTIAL PSYCHOLOGICAL EVALUATION
JANE Q. PATIENT
SEPTEMBER 21, 2001

ing and spelling. On a separate test of visuomotor integration, Ms. Patient exhibited mild deficits, likely the result of observable tremulousness.

Overall, in terms of intellectual and cognitive functioning, Ms. Patient scored within the Average Range of intelligence which likely is an underestimate of her potential, given emotional factors and the effects of medication. Her verbal abilities, including vocabulary, were well above average, and she exhibited some motor slowness, likely the result of psychomotor retardation and/or problems with concentration. On a screening test of academic performance, she scored on a college level for both reading and spelling. Screening for possible central nervous system impairment was negative.

PERSONALITY FUNCTIONING: Ms. Patient was well oriented. During the evaluation, she exhibited flat affect, or emotional level, for the most part. Her speech was hesitant and slow and, as indicated above, she exhibited some psychomotor retardation, some of which may be due to the effects of medication. She exhibited periods of tearfulness when discussing her life circumstance, especially relationship issues. Ms. Patient's speech was logical and coherent and she did not exhibit indications of looseness of associations, tangential thinking, or pressured speech. She experienced problems with concentration. Assessment did not reveal indications of psychosis, underlying or overt. She denied current hallucinations both visual and auditory; however, she did report that she has heard a voice in the past of a degrading nature, telling her "You don't deserve to live." She stated that the voice is that of a female and that it comes from inside her head. Ms. Patient did not exhibit delusional thinking during the assessment, and collateral information does not support the existence of past delusional thought. She reported that she has been feeling depressed and sleeping much of the time. She also reported that her appetite is "too good" and she has little interest in activity of any type. Ms. Patient denied current suicidal and homicidal ideation, although she reported that she has had self-destructive thinking as recent as the day prior to this examination.

On an intrapsychic level, assessment revealed that Ms. Patient experiences problems integrating emotional experience; that is, she is sometimes overwhelmed by her emotions to the extent that she is unable to think clearly. She reported significant feelings of depression and on projective assessment Ms.

PAGE #
CONFIDENTIAL PSYCHOLOGICAL EVALUATION
JANE Q. PATIENT
SEPTEMBER 21, 2001

Patient produced themes of sadness. She admits to problems with emotional control (i.e., periods of crying and anger). On exploration, Ms. Patient reported that she sometimes wakes up in the morning and "I feel like breaking something." Ms. Patient tends to deny and minimize the extent of her problems and resulting emotional unrest. These feelings build and are discharged in a sometimes uncontrolled manner. Ms. Patient tends to take a passive stance to her anger, internalizing her feelings, which results in depression. She often feels remorseful and guilty about her behaviors in an intropunitive manner. This results in feelings of self-rejection and self-destructive ideation. Ms. Patient has a strong need to be seen in a positive light by others. This not only serves to compensate for feelings of inadequacy but also serves as a defense mechanism (reaction formation) to protect against the expression of hostile impulses which she would consider unacceptable. Her auditory hallucinations, which are of a self-condemning nature, act as a form of self-punishment. Although Ms. Patient has a strong need to be seen in a positive light by others, she also has a need to be viewed as having severe emotional problems. This allows her to rationalize to herself and others the lack of meeting her own internal standards and her passive stance. Assessment revealed that Ms. Patient is pessimistic about the future with little hope of her life improving. Her thoughts about herself are of a negative nature and maintain her passive and self-deprecating posture. All of this contributes to frustration, confusion, and an extremely poor self-image. Although Ms. Patient denies current self-destructive intent, the above psychological symptoms and dynamics are indicative of significant risk for self-destructive behavior in the future. While Ms. Patient does exhibit some insight into her problems, recognizing she experiences significant difficulty with depression, she does not realize that she contributes to her own problems via her negative thought patterns and passivity.

On an interpersonal level, Ms. Patient relates in a passive-dependent fashion. She resents her dependency upon her parents but feels inadequate to separate from them. Although she desires to please her parents, she believes that she has not met their expectations for her and projects feelings of rejection onto them. Personality assessment indicated that Ms. Patient feels alienated from her family and from society in general. She does not feel that she is part of any social group and believes she is viewed as inferior by others. Ms. Patient feels uncomfortable in social settings and tends to withdraw and isolate. She experiences considerable anxiety about relating to the opposite sex. Her hostility and inappropriate behaviors (e.g., self-destruction and social avoidance) result in rejection by others. This rejection serves to reinforce her underlying hypothesis about herself that she is inferior, and adds to feelings of lack of self-worth.

IMPRESSIONS: Overall, Ms. Patient appears to be experiencing significant feelings of depression with periodic psychotic symptoms which seem to be consistent with her depressed mood. Assessment did not support the existence of severe personality disorganization or a major psychosis. She also exhibits dependent personality characteristics and has experienced problems with substance abuse/dependance.

SUMMARY: Ms. Patient is a 28-year-old, Caucasian, single female who has been referred for psychological evaluation to assist in differentiating between major depression and psychosis. She is currently hospitalized following an attempted suicide. Ms. Patient was well oriented to time, person, and place. She also was well aware of the circumstances under which she was evaluated. On the test of intelligence, she scored within the Average Range although it is estimated that her potential level of intellect is within the High Average Range. On a screening test of academic achievement, she scored at a college level for both reading and spelling. Assessment revealed indications of psychomotor retardation, probably due to emotional factors and/or the effects of medication. This likely had a negative impact on her performance on the test of intelligence; it is estimated that Ms. Patient's potential level of intellect falls within the High Average Range. Screening measures for neuropsychological dysfunction did not indicate impairment. Assessment did not reveal that Ms. Patient was experiencing a psychosis, and her perception of reality appeared generally intact. However, there were indications that, when stressed, she may exhibit psychotic symptoms (auditory hallucinations) consistent with her depressed mood. When overwhelmed with emotion, her thinking becomes confused. Ms. Patient appears to be experiencing depression of major proportion. This depression also seems to be relatively longstanding. Assessment also revealed underlying hostility and feelings of a lack of self-worth. Interpersonally, she relates in a hostile-dependent manner. She tends to repress unwanted emotions and project feelings of rejection onto others. Ms. Patient also tends to isolate and withdraw from social contact. Although she denies current sui-

PAGE #
CONFIDENTIAL PSYCHOLOGICAL EVALUATION
JANE Q. PATIENT
SEPTEMBER 21, 2001

cidal and homicidal ideation, she has tried to harm herself in the recent past and assessment reveals self-destructive tendencies.

RECOMMENDATIONS: Ms. Patient was cooperative during the evaluation session and completed all tasks asked of her. Although she did not appear to be experiencing a major mental illness that would significantly distort her perception of reality, there were indications of considerable emotional conflict. Problem areas, along with strengths, are discussed below with recommendations.

1.   *General Psychological Functioning:* At the time of this assessment, Ms. Patient did not appear to be experiencing psychosis with significant personality disorganization. However, assessment did reveal that she has been experiencing a major mental illness for some time which appears to be a recurrent Major Depression with psychotic features. Given the degree of her depression and self-destructive behavior, continued hospitalization and stabilization of her mood is recommended at this time. Ongoing evaluation and monitoring of her medication is imperative. Continued individual psychotherapy is also recommended to address her depression, social withdrawal, and lack of activity in her life. A cognitive-behavioral approach to this may prove beneficial. It is also recommended that she be supported in the constructive expression of anger and that her destructive hostile behaviors be addressed through anger management.

2.   *Educational/Vocational Issues:* Ms. Patient was, reportedly, a good student while she was attending school. She completed 2 years of college but left school for "emotional" reasons. On the test of intelligence, she scored within the Average Range, although psychological factors, as well as the effects of medication, likely lowered her score. It is estimated that her potential level of intelligence is within the High Average Range. On a screening test of academic achievement, she scored at a college level for both reading and spelling. Given these scores, Ms. Patient appears to have the potential to perform well in educational/training pursuits. Also, when she was employed, she had been described as a reliable employee who performed well. It is recommended that these strengths be integrated into her treatment as a means of increasing her sense of positive self-esteem. Assisting Ms. Patient in developing vocational/educational goals is recommended.

PAGE #
CONFIDENTIAL PSYCHOLOGICAL EVALUATION
JANE Q. PATIENT
SEPTEMBER 21, 2001

3. *Lack of Treatment Compliance:* Ms. Patient has not been compliant with treatment in the past, both in terms of taking prescribed medication and attendance to therapy. It is recommended that this lack of compliance be explored with her in therapy, as it relates to possible resistance/passive-aggressive behavior. It is imperative that she remain medication compliant and develop an emotional investment in therapy.

4. *Substance Abuse:* Ms. Patient appears to have a history of substance abuse/dependence. Her substance of choice has been alcohol. She likely has used substances as a means of self-medicating her depression. Alcohol consumption can have a negative impact on medication effectiveness and retard psychological growth. Alcohol use can also negatively affect judgment, disinhibit emotional controls, and contribute to central nervous system damage. It is recommended that Ms. Patient participate in services to address her substance involvement and to monitor closely for use/abuse, especially alcohol. If use is suspected, random drug screens may be appropriate to monitor for use and to assist with determining level of denial.

5. *Suicidal Ideation/Behavior:* Ms. Patient has exhibited suicidal behavior on at least three known occasions. Her last suicide attempt appeared serious and was relatively recent. She cut her wrist deeply requiring several sutures. Although she currently denies any self-destructive intent, her depression and history of attempts to harm herself places her at risk for future self-destructive behavior. It is recommended that she be monitored closely for suicidal ideation and that she remain compliant with her medication. It is also recommended that self-destructive tendencies be explored with her in therapy as well as developing means to identify when she begins to experience self-destructive thoughts. Alternative behaviors to self-harm and cognitive intervention may prove beneficial. Given her recent suicidal attempt and level of current depression, continued hospitalization is recommended at this time.

6. *Social Withdrawal and Lack of Activity:* Ms. Patient, as stated above and prior to her suicide attempt, was reportedly withdrawn and isolated. In addition, she had not been involved in any known positive activity. It is recommended that behavior shaping be employed to address this issue. Given that she reportedly functioned well when she was working, voca-

PAGE #
CONFIDENTIAL PSYCHOLOGICAL EVALUATION
JANE Q. PATIENT
SEPTEMBER 21, 2001

tional pursuits may also help with socialization. Reports revealed that Ms. Patient has had an interest in music, which could be another possible avenue for activity. Exploration of relationship issues is also recommended along with assessment of her social skills and thinking about herself concerning social withdrawal as well as lack of positive activity.

7. *Dependency Issues:* Psychological assessment indicated that Ms. Patient is dependent on her parents but that she resents this dependency. This contributes to her hostility. Exploration of issues of autonomy versus dependency in therapy is recommended with the goal of Ms. Patient achieving independent functioning to the extent appropriate.

_____
N. O. Question, PhD
Clinical Psychologist

NOQ/dlf

REFERENCES

CITED REFERENCES

American Psychiatric Association. (1980). *A Psychiatric Glossary* (5th ed.). Boston: Little, Brown & Company.

American Psychiatric Association. (2000). *Diagnostic and Statistical Manual of Mental Disorders* (4th ed., text revision). Washington, DC: Author.

American Psychological Association. (1992). Ethical principles of psychologists and code of conduct. *American Psychologist, 47*(12), 390-395.

Applebaum, S. A. (1972). A method of reporting psychological test findings. *Bulletin of the Menninger Clinic, 36*(5), 535-545.

Auger, T. J. (1974). Mental health terminology - A modern tower of Babel? *Journal of Community Psychology, 2*(2), 113-116.

Axelrod, B. N. (2000). Neuropsychological report writing. In R. D. Vanderploeg (Ed.), *Clinicians Guide to Neuropsychological Assessment* (pp. 245-273). Mahwah, NJ: Lawrence Erlbaum.

Beck, A. T. (1978). *Beck Depression Inventory.* San Antonio, TX: The Psychological Corporation.

Bender, L. (1938). *A Visual Motor Gestalt Test and Its Clinical Use.* New York: The American Orthopsychiatric Association.

Bowen, M. (1961). The family as the unit of study and treatment. *American Journal of Psychiatry, 31,* 50-60.

Carson, R. C. (1990). Assessment: What role the assessor? *Journal of Personality Assessment, 54*(3 & 4), 435-445.

Exner, J. E., Jr. (1986). *The Rorschach: A Comprehensive System* (2nd ed.). New York: John Wiley & Sons.

Fowler, R. D., & Butcher, J. N. (1986). Critique to Matarazzo's views on computerized testing: All sigma and no meaning. *American Psychologist, 41,* 94-96.

Golden, C. J., Purisch, A. D., & Hammeke, T. A. (1985). *Manual: Luria-Nebraska Neuropsychological Battery: Form I and II.* Los Angeles, CA: Western Psychological Services.

Hartlage, L. C., & Merck, K. H. (1971). Increasing the relevance of psychological reports. *Journal of Clinical Psychology, 27*(4), 459-460.

Harvey, V. S. (1997). Improving the readability of psychological reports. *Professional Psychology: Research, Theory and Practice, 28*(3), 271-274.

Hathaway, S. R., & McKinley, J. C. (1989). *Minnesota Multiphasic Personality Inventory-2.* Minneapolis, MN: University of Minnesota Press.

Heaton, R. K., Chelune, G. J., Kay, G. G., & Curtiss, G. (1993). *Wisconsin Card Sorting Test Manual: Revised and Expanded.* Odessa, FL: Psychological Assessment Resources.

Hollis, J. W., & Donn, P. A. (1979). *Psychological Report Writing: Theory and Practice.* Muncie, IN: Accelerated Development.

Hooper, H. E. (1983). *Hooper Visual Organization Test (VOT).* Los Angeles, CA: Western Psychological Services.

Jones, R. L., & Gross, F. P. (1959). The readability of psychological reports. *American Journal of Mental Deficiency, 63,* 1020-1021.

Kendall, B. S. (1962). Memory-for-designs performance in the seventh and eighth decades of life. *Perceptual and Motor Skills, 14,* 399-405.

Klopher, W. G. (1960). *The Psychological Report: Use and Communication of Psychological Findings.* New York: Grune & Stratton.

Leary, T. (1957). *Interpersonal Diagnosis of Personality: A Functional Theory and Methodology for Personality Evaluation.* New York: John Wiley & Sons.

Levin, H. S., & Spiers, P. A. (1985). Acalculia. In K. M. Heilman & E. Valenstein (Eds.), *Clinical Neuropsychology* (2nd ed., pp. 97-114). New York: Oxford University Press.

Lezak, M. D. (1983). *Neuropsychological Assessment* (2nd ed.). New York: Oxford University Press.

Lodge, G. T. (1953). How to write a psychological report. *Journal of Clinical Psychology, 9,* 400-402.

Matarazzo, J. D. (1983). Computerized psychological testing. *Science, 221,* 232.

Matarazzo, J. D. (1986a). Computerized clinical psychological test interpretations: Unvalidated plus all men and no signa. *American Psychologist, 41,* 14-24.

Matarazzo, J. D. (1986b). Response to Fowler and Butcher on Matarazzo. *American Psychologist, 41,* 96.

Mayman, M. (1959). Style, focus, language and content of an ideal psychological test report. *Journal of Projective Techniques and Personality Assessment, 23,* 453-458.

Menninger, W. C. (1948). Psychiatry and psychology. *American Journal of Psychiatry, 105,* 389-390.

Millon, T. F. (1994). *Millon Clinical Multiaxial Inventory-III: Manual.* Minneapolis, MN: National Computer Systems.

Morey, C. L. (1992). *Personality Assessment Inventory.* Odessa, FL: Psychological Assessment Resources.

Murray, H. A. (1943). *Thematic Apperception Test Manual.* Cambridge, MA: Harvard University Press.

Ownby, R. L. (1991). *Psychological Reports: A Guide to Report Writing in Professional Psychology* (2nd ed.). Brandon, VT: Clinical Psychology Publishing Company.

Ownby, R. L. (1997). *Psychological Report Writing: A Guide to Writing in Professional Psychology* (3rd ed.). New York: John Wiley & Sons.

The Psychological Corporation. (1992). *Wechsler Individual Achievement Test Manual.* San Antonio, TX: Author.

The Psychological Corporation. (1999). *Wechsler Abbreviated Scale of Intelligence.* San Antonio, TX: Author.

Rabin, A. I. (1981). *Assessment With Projective Techniques: A Concise Introduction.* New York: Springer.

Reitan, R. M., & Wolfson, D. (1985). *The Halstead-Reitan Neuropsychological Test Battery: Theory and Clinical Interpretation.* Tucson, AZ: Neuropsychology Press.

Rorschach, H. (1948). *Rorschach: Psychodiagnostics.* New York: Grune & Stratton.

Sullivan, H. S. (1947). *Conceptions of Modern Psychiatry.* Washington, DC: The William Alanson White Psychiatric Foundation.

Tallent, N. (1980). *Report Writing in Special Education*. Englewood Cliffs, NJ: Prentice-Hall.

Tallent, N. (1993). *Psychological Report Writing*. Upper Saddle River, NJ: Prentice-Hall.

Tallent, N., & Reiss, W. J. (1959a). Multidisciplinary views of the preparation of written clinical psychological reports: I. Spontaneous suggestions for content. *Journal of Clinical Psychology, 15,* 218-221.

Wechsler, D. (1974). *Wechsler Intelligence Scale for Children-Third Revision*. San Antonio, TX: The Psychological Corporation.

Wechsler, D. (1981). *Wechsler Adult Intelligence Scale-Revised*. San Antonio, TX: The Psychological Corporation.

Wechsler, D. (1989). *Wechsler Preschool and Primary Scale of Intelligence-Revised*. San Antonio, TX: The Psychological Corporation.

Wechsler, D. (1997). *Wechsler Adult Intelligence Scale, Third Edition*. San Antonio, TX: The Psychological Corporation.

Weiner, J. (1985). Teacher's comprehension of psychological reports. *Psychology in the Schools, 22*(1), 60-64.

Weiner, I. B. (1999). Writing forensic reports. In A. K. Hess & I. B. Weiner (Eds.), *The Handbook of Forensic Psychology* (2nd ed.). New York: John Wiley & Sons.

Wilkinson, G. S. (1993). *Wide Range Achievement Test-Revision 3*. Wilmington, DE: Jastac Associates/Wide Range Inc.

Wolber, G. J. (1980). A practical approach to the psychological evaluation of elderly patients. *Perceptual and Motor Skills, 51,* 499-505.

Wolber, G. J., & Carne, W. F. (1993). *Writing Psychological Reports: A Guide for Clinicians*. Sarasota, FL: Professional Resource Press.

ADDITIONAL REFERENCES

Cattell, R. B., Eber, H. W., & Tatsuoka, M. M. (1970). *Sixteen Personality Factor Questionnaire*. Champaign, IL: Institute for Personality and Ability Testing.

Heilman, K. M., & Valenstein, E. (Eds.). (1985). *Clinical Neuropsychology* (2nd ed.). New York: Oxford University Press.

Kaplan, H. C., & Sadock, B. J. (Eds.). (1985). *Comprehensive Textbook of Psychiatry* (4th ed.). Baltimore, MD: Williams & Wilkins.

Piotrowski, Z. A. (1937). The Rorschach Inkblot method in organic disturbance of the central nervous system. *Journal of Nervous and Mental Diseases, 86,* 525-537.

Richman, J. (1967). Reporting diagnostic test results to patients and their families. *Journal of Projective Techniques and Personality Assessment, 31,* 62-70.

Sternberg, R. J. (1977). *Writing the Psychology Paper.* New York: Barron's Educational Series.

Tallent, N., & Reiss, W. J. (1959b). Multidisciplinary views of the preparation of written clinical psychological reports: II. Acceptability of certain common content variables and styles of expression. *Journal of Clinical Psychology, 15,* 273-274.

Wolber, G. J., & Banze, B. (1997). The assessment and management of problematic areas contributing to recidivism of adolescent adult offenders. *Juvenile and Family Court Journal, 49*(1), 1-9.

Wolman, B. B. (Ed.). (1973). *Dictionary of Behavioral Science.* New York: Van Nostrand Reinhold.

SUBJECT INDEX

Add A Colleague To Our Mailing List . . .

If you would like us to send our latest catalog to one of your colleagues, please return this form:

Name: _____
(Please Print)

Address: _____

Address: _____

City/State/Zip: _____
This is   ☐ home   ☐ office

Telephone: (_____)_____

E-mail: _____

Fax: (_____) _____

This person is a:

☐   Psychologist   ☐   Mental Health Counselor
☐   Psychiatrist   ☐   Marriage and Family Therapist
☐   School Psychologist   ☐   Not in Mental Health Field
☐   Clinical Social Worker   ☐   Other: _____

Name of person completing this form: _____

◆   ◆   ◆

Professional Resource Press
P.O. Box 15560
Sarasota, FL 34277-1560

Telephone: 800-443-3364
FAX: 941-343-9201
E-mail: mail@prpress.com
Website: http://www.prpress.com

If You Found This Book Useful . . .

You might want to know more about our other titles.

If you would like to receive our latest catalog, please return this form:

Name: _____
(Please Print)

Address: _____

Address: _____

City/State/Zip: _____
This is ☐ home ☐ office

Telephone: (_____)_____

E-mail: _____

Fax: (_____) _____

I am a:

☐ Psychologist   ☐ Mental Health Counselor
☐ Psychiatrist   ☐ Marriage and Family Therapist
☐ School Psychologist   ☐ Not in Mental Health Field
☐ Clinical Social Worker   ☐ Other: _____

◆   ◆   ◆

Professional Resource Press
P.O. Box 15560
Sarasota, FL 34277-1560

Telephone: 800-443-3364
FAX: 941-343-9201
E-mail: mail@prpress.com
Website: http://www.prpress.com